538144

D1253625

DISCARD
DISCARD

RA...E S
BURNETT

'95

DISCARD
DISCARD

Frances Hodgson Burnett

Twayne's English Authors Series

Herbert Sussman, Editor

Northeastern University

TEAS 373

CHAMPLAIN COLLEGE

DISCARD
DISCARD

FRANCES HODGSON BURNETT
(1849–1924)
Photograph reproduced by permission of
The Huntington Library, San Marino, California

Frances Hodgson Burnett

By Phyllis Bixler
Kansas State University

Twayne Publishers • Boston

Frances Hodgson Burnett

Phyllis Bixler

Copyright © 1984 by G. K. Hall & Company
All Rights Reserved
Published by Twayne Publishers
A Division of G. K. Hall & Company
70 Lincoln Street
Boston, Massachusetts 02111

Book Production by Marne B. Sultz

Book Design by Barbara Anderson

Printed on permanent/durable acid-free
paper and bound in the United States of
America.

Library of Congress Cataloging in Publication Data

Bixler, Phyllis.
    Frances Hodgson Burnett

    (Twayne's English authors series ; TEAS 373)
    Bibliography: p. 136
    Includes index.
    1. Burnett, Frances Hodgson, 1849–1924—Criticism
and interpretation.   I. Title.   II. Series.
PS1217.B59   1984   813.'4   84-661
ISBN 0-8057-6859-9

For my family, George and Martha Bixler;
George, Anita, Jeff, Andy, and Steve Bixler

Contents

About the Author

Phyllis Bixler received her B.A. from Bluffton College, Bluffton, Ohio, and her M.A. and Ph.D. from the University of Kansas. She is an associate professor of English at Kansas State University and has published articles on children's literature as well as several on Burnett, including "Tradition and the Individual Talent of Frances Hodgson Burnett," which won the 1980 Literary Criticism Award from the Children's Literature Association. She is now completing a book, *The Child in the Garden: Pastoral Ideals in Rousseau, Wordsworth, and Children's Literature.*

Preface

Frances Hodgson Burnett is now chiefly known as a children's writer, even though during her publishing career of over fifty-five years most of her fiction was intended for adults. *The Secret Garden* (1911), justifiably regarded as her masterpiece for children, has received the most critical attention. *Little Lord Fauntleroy* (1886), for which she was most famous during her lifetime, still has wide title recognition if probably fewer readers. For many, the name of Burnett's child paragon connotes foppish clothes and sentimentality about children; and his story has been kept alive in the popular imagination through four movie adaptations from 1914 to 1980. *A Little Princess* (1905) completes the trio of Burnett's best-known and best books for children, though *The Lost Prince* (1915) also finds appreciative readers. The following study will pay special attention to these books as well as to the considerable body of Burnett's lesser-known literature for and about the child, particularly her childhood memoir, *The One I Knew the Best of All* (1893).

Significant attention will also be given to Burnett's fiction for adults. Before the phenomenal international popularity of *Little Lord Fauntleroy* established Burnett's career as a children's author, she gained a justifiable reputation in both Britain and America as a promising writer of adult novels. *That Lass o' Lowrie's* (1877) and *Haworth's* (1879), industrial novels set in Burnett's native Lancashire, continued the tradition of British social and political fiction established in the 1840s and 1850s by writers such as Elizabeth Gaskell, Charlotte Brontë, Benjamin Disraeli, and Charles Dickens. In *Through One Administration* (1883), set in contemporary Washington, D.C., Burnett chose as models Henry Adams, William Dean Howells, and especially Henry James.

Most of Burnett's adult fiction, however, belongs to the general category of the popular romance. Largely self-educated, Burnett learned her craft while writing formulaic stories for magazines such as *Godey's Lady's Book, Peterson's Ladies' Magazine,* and eventually the more prestigious *Scribner's Monthly.* When she moved from short fiction to romance, audiences on both sides of the Atlantic rewarded her with wealth and fame. After *Little Lord Fauntleroy,* she produced at least one best-seller every decade through the 1920s, and Francis J. Molson estimates that she derived from her writing an income greater than any of her British or American contemporaries.[1]

Though now read by few, Burnett's popular adult fiction deserves critical attention because it sheds light on her better-known children's fiction and because it provides insights into the nature of popular fiction and how it might be appropriately evaluated. In writing for children, Burnett adapted character types and plot formulas she used first in her popular fiction for adults; and her children's fiction, like her popular adult fiction, belongs not to the tradition of the realist novel but to that of the romance. Burnett's romances for both audiences often rely on the folktale for their plots and themes; and they resemble the folktale also in their method of eliciting audience satisfaction. Broadly speaking, the realist novel often tries to obscure the literary conventions it uses in order to convince the reader that life is being portrayed as we daily experience it rather than as traditionally portrayed in fiction. Burnett's romances, like the folktale, however, are often frankly formulaic and thus advertise themselves as fiction; they aim to satisfy not so much our sense of how life is but rather our desires about what it might be. The aesthetic achievement of such romances is therefore measured much as is an oral retelling or written version of a folktale—by the author's ability to embroider, vary, or in some minor way deviate from the familiar formulas just enough to intensify, without fundamentally altering, the audience's expected enjoyment of those formulas, as John G. Cawelti has pointed out.[2] Burnett proved a master of this art in her best children's books as well as in several of her popular adult romances, notably *The Making of a Marchioness* (1901) and *T. Tembarom* (1913), all variations of the Cinderella tale.

Burnett's popular adult fiction is of interest also because of her treatment of certain social themes which, if undoubtedly handled more effectively by authors of greater stature, nevertheless provides insights as to how these issues were made accessible to a large proportion of the reading public. In approaching Burnett's presentation of these themes, it is again helpful to compare popular fiction to the folktale, both of which, like children's literature, have an important social as well as aesthetic function. Like the folktale in oral cultures, popular adult fiction and much of children's fiction serve both to pass on traditional values and to help society accommodate change. As Cawelti has pointed out,[3] the familiar formulas give the reader a sense of continuity with the past and create a reassuring sense of order. Within the safety provided by adherence to these formulas, new ideas or social realities can be cautiously explored. Such interjections of the new as well as controlled touches of realism typically provide most of the variations of familiar formulas in popular fiction. Since society frequently absorbs "new" ideas which then become truisms, and since those conservative checks, literary formulas, themselves sometimes change, much popular fiction soon seems dated. Often, however, such fiction proves instructive to the social and literary historian, especially that of an author like Burnett whose popularity spanned almost six decades.

Contemporary concerns reflected in Burnett's popular fiction include the impact of Darwin's theory of evolution; late-nineteenth-century religious movements such as theosophy and Christian Science; contrasts and interrelationships between British and American societies; social disruptions caused by World War I; and changing roles for women. This last issue engaged Burnett in some of her early, realist fiction as well as in much of her later, popular fiction; and a concern for specifically female sources of power surfaced in some of her children's fiction as well, especially *The Secret Garden.*

Because of Burnett's preoccupation with female roles in her fiction, and because Burnett's own life and career resembled those of a considerable number of contemporary female writers, the following critical study will discuss Burnett's contributions to the female tradition in British and American literature as well as to children's literature, the realist novel, and the popular romance. As Elaine Showalter has pointed out, Burnett belonged to the first generation of women writers to exploit rather than play down "the commercial, competitive, self-promoting aspects . . . of literary life."[4] Eminently successful in promoting her career, Burnett, and undoubtedly others like her, bore the double stigma of having broken traditional female roles in her life and of having debased herself in her career by writing popular fiction. This double stigma often kept Burnett's considerable literary achievements from being recognized during her lifetime and after, as Molson pointed out in his 1975 call for a reassessment of Burnett's career.[5] The following chronological and critical survey of Burnett's fiction for children and adults attempts such a reassessment.

Phyllis Bixler

Kansas State University

Acknowledgments

Most of what I owe to others must be cited in my notes and bibliography. Here, however, I want to acknowledge special debts to two who have studied Burnett before me. Francis J. Molson's 1975 survey of Burnett's critical reception and his interpretations of Burnett's fiction have benefitted me greatly, and I cannot thank him enough for his personal and professional support of my undertaking this project. I am also deeply indebted to Ann Thwaite's 1974 biography of Burnett. Most of my information about Burnett's life comes from Thwaite's book as does my description of Burnett's theatrical career, which could not be surveyed fully within the following study of her considerable body of fiction. Also, I have often relied on Thwaite's bibliography for information about first editions of Burnett's books, especially those in Great Britain. Without the help of Thwaite's work, my own study would have been much longer in the making. I am very grateful to her.

Two institutions and their personnel have given me support for which I offer thanks. The Huntington Library, San Marino, California, gave me a 1979 Summer Fellowship as well as permission to reproduce the photograph of Burnett for a frontispiece. From Kansas State University I received a 1981 Summer Faculty Research Grant; other monetary support for research expenses; some release from classroom duties, allowed by the English Department head, Richard McGhee; and assistance from the English Department secretarial staff, especially Billie Tunison and Carolyn Everett.

I also appreciate the professional encouragement and criticism given me on this project by my Twayne editor, Herbert Sussman, and more generally by colleagues within the Children's Literature Association, especially Lois Kuznets, Sonja Landes, Anita Moss, Jon Stott, and Virginia Wolf. I thank Clayton Koppes for his early encouragement of my interest in Burnett. For sustaining and diverting me as I was writing, and for valuable rereadings of my manuscript, I owe much to Lucien Agosta.

Chronology

1849   Frances Hodgson born Manchester, England, 24 November.

1865   Moves to New Market, Tennessee.

1868   Publishes first stories, in *Godey's Lady's Book*.

1873   Marries Dr. Swan Burnett, 19 September, in Tennessee.

1874   Son Lionel born, 20 September, in Tennessee.

1876   Son Vivian born, 5 April, in Paris.

1877   *That Lass o' Lowrie's; Surly Tim and Other Stories*. Moves to Washington, D.C.

1879   *Haworth's*. Publishes first of many stories in *St. Nicholas Magazine*.

1880   *Louisiana;* "Editha's Burglar" in *St. Nicholas*.

1881   *A Fair Barbarian*.

1883   *Through One Administration*.

1886   *Little Lord Fauntleroy*.

1887   "Sara Crewe" in *St. Nicholas; A Woman's Will* (England), or *Miss Defarge* (United States, 1888). Attends Queen Victoria's Jubilee in London and for the next twenty-five years maintains residences in England and sometimes in Italy as well as in the United States.

1888   *The Real Little Lord Fauntleroy,* play, opens in London and New York.

1889   *The Pretty Sister of José*.

1890   *Little Saint Elizabeth and Other Stories. Nixie* (from "Editha's Burglar") opens in London, establishing a decade of theatrical collaboration and close friendship with Stephen Townesend. Son Lionel dies.

1892   *Giovanni and the Other* (United States), or *Children I Have Known* (England).

1893   *The One I Knew the Best of All*.

1894   *Piccino and Other Child Stories*.

1895　*Two Little Pilgrims' Progress.*

1896　*A Lady of Quality.*

1898　Divorces Swan Burnett. Begins nine-year residence at May-tham Hall, Rolvenden, Kent.

1899　*In Connection with The De Willoughby Claim.*

1900　Marries Stephen Townesend, February, in Genoa, Italy.

1901　*The Making of a Marchioness* and *The Methods of Lady Walderhurst.*

1902　*A Little Princess,* play, opens in London (in New York, 1903). Breaks with Stephen Townesend.

1904　*In the Closed Room.*

1905　*A Little Princess,* book. Becomes United States citizen.

1906　*Racketty-Packetty House.*

1907　*The Shuttle.*

1909　Moves into new home at Plandome, Long Island.

1911　*The Secret Garden.*

1912　*Racketty-Packetty House,* play, opens in New York.

1913　*T. Tembarom.*

1914　Last return to the United States. Spends most of rest of her life at Plandome and on Bermuda.

1915　*The Lost Prince.*

1917　*The White People* (United States; England, 1920).

1922　*The Head of the House of Coombe* and *Robin.*

1924　Burnett dies at Plandome, Long Island, 29 October.

Chapter One
The Woman and the Writer

Principal themes in the fiction of Frances Hodgson Burnett were forecast in seven books published within two years of her birth, on 24 November 1849, in Manchester, England; and the authors of these works would be among the most important in shaping her fiction. Charlotte Brontë's *Jane Eyre* (1847), Emily Brontë's *Wuthering Heights* (1847), and Charles Dickens's *David Copperfield* (1849–50) offered pioneering fictional portrayals of childhood, and the works for which Burnett would eventually be best known were written for and about children. Elizabeth Gaskell's *Mary Barton* (1848) and Charlotte Brontë's *Shirley* (1849) depicted industrial strife and the life and language of laboring people; Burnett would also choose these subjects for fiction set in her adopted America as well as in England, and this realist fiction would by 1883 bring her critical acclaim as a promising young novelist. Finally, William Makepeace Thackeray's *Vanity Fair* (1847–48) and Gaskell's *Cranford* (1851–53) demonstrated the interest in documenting social life at its hub and in the provinces that Burnett would display throughout her career. The long romances of social life she wrote during the last twenty-five years of her life sold especially well. However, by the time she died, on 29 October 1924, novels by authors such as James Joyce, Virginia Woolf, Ernest Hemingway, and F. Scott Fitzgerald made Burnett seem to critics and other readers a "relic of Victorianism."[1]

Childhood and Youth in England and America

The circumstances of Burnett's childhood and youth also foreshadowed much of her later life and fiction.[2] The many radical changes of fortune experienced by her fictional characters were no doubt prompted by literary convention, but these changes must have had special meaning for an author who during her first sixteen years went from the sheltered household of a prosperous Manchester tradesman to almost penniless dependence on an uncle, in rural Tennessee. Edwin Hodgson's successful business selling household furnishings to

Manchester's moneyed aristocracy allowed him to give his wife, Eliza Boond Hodgson, and their five children a comfortable suburban home.

This family security was undermined, however, when Edwin died in 1853, four months before his last child was born. Eliza bravely undertook management of her dead husband's business; but during the next ten years the Manchester economy plummetted, largely because the American Civil War hindered the shipments of cotton needed by the city's textile industry. New houses were no longer built, and the Hodgson General Furnishing Business suffered accordingly. Finally, Eliza sold the business and in 1865 took her family to Tennessee, where her brother had earlier settled. The changes of these early years were prophetic of Burnett's international life—she would cross the Atlantic thirty-three times and reside almost equal amounts of time in England and America. Also, her parents' Manchester business was reiterated in her lifelong delight in furnishing and refurnishing the houses marking her own changing fortunes and identities.

That the contrasts in her several childhood residences made a deep impression on young Burnett is indicated by her memoir, *The One I Knew the Best of All* (1893). She especially remembered Seedley Grove, a comfortable, suburban house owned by relatives, where Burnett's widowed mother took her family while she looked for a house she could afford. Frances was then five, and she remembered the back yard of Seedley as a "Garden of Eden" where the sun always shone. It rarely seemed to shine in Islington Square where the family moved in 1855; instead, Burnett remembered the smuts that continually rained down from factory chimneys near this island of dilapidated gentility surrounded by overcrowded houses of millworkers. Always admonished to act and speak like a "lady," Frances was not allowed to play with the mill-workers' children. But she was fascinated by the glimpses of another kind of life she saw just outside the square. Presaging the use of dialect in some of her fiction, the young Frances loved and became fluent in the forbidden Lancashire dialect the street children spoke. The contrast between those ten years in smoky, crowded Manchester and the following three years of relative isolation in rural Tennessee could hardly be greater. Burnett described this latter period, when she was sixteen through nineteen, as her "Dryad Days." The intense love of nature she discovered here would surface in the pastoral themes of works such as *The Secret Garden* as well as in her passion for gardening during the last twenty-five years of her life.

Glorious afternoons in the Tennessee thicket she called her "Bower," however, did not change the family's poverty—they often had barely enough to eat; and increasingly, teenaged Burnett felt herself responsible for improving the family fortune. Raising geese and establishing a "Select Seminary" alike failed. Finally, Burnett hit upon the money-making method that would eventually bring her great wealth. For thirty-five dollars she sold her first two stories, published in *Godey's Lady's Book* in 1868, when she was nineteen. During the next three years, she later reported, she had stories published "in every magazine in America, except *Harper's, Scribner's,* and the *Atlantic,*" and others devoted to the "actual literature" she regarded as beyond her powers.[3]

Much of Burnett's childhood memoir describes personality traits and experiences that led to this early publishing success. From earliest memory, Burnett loved stories. Her only formal education was a dame school in Manchester, and so most of her reading was done outside school assignments, a self-educating process that would continue throughout her life. Burnett lists Sir Walter Scott, Harrison Ainsworth, Mayne Reid, and James Fenimore Cooper as favorite childhood authors, but her love for adventure led her also to Greek, Roman, and British histories and mythologies. At age seven she discovered a bound volume of *Blackwood's* which led to a continuing preoccupation with fiction in magazines such as *Young Ladies' Halfpenny Journal, Cornhill, Temple Bar, London Society, Godey's Lady's Book,* and *Peterson's.* From these, Burnett quickly learned the formulas of plot and style she used to spin long, oral tales for her schoolmates and to write stories she shared with her mother and sister Edith. By the time she submitted a story to *Godey's Lady's Book,* she had mastered the conventions of British ladies' magazine fiction so well that *Godey's* editor, Sara Lucretia Hale, questioned whether the story was "original" with the author from Tennessee. Frances had to write another story to convince her.

These childhood experiences hint at some reasons for her later productivity and popularity as a writer. Her ability to quickly master literary conventions helps explain the frequent ease and speed with which she wrote, and in a variety of genres—short fiction, essays, novels, romances, adaptations for the stage. Her popularity in part grew from the desire and ability to please an audience which she showed in her early story-telling performances. She continued to use oral methods in her writing process and to value her audience's response; she would compose a story orally before writing it, or, as she was writing, she would read selected pages aloud to family, friends, or editor, using the response to guide what followed. Her childhood story performances revealed another trait which undoubtedly led to her popularity as a writer—her predilection for stories which, like fairy stories, have a happy ending. In the stories she told classmates during their "Embroidery Afternoons," "penitant lovers were always forgiven, rash ones were reconciled, wickedness was always punished, offended relatives always relented . . . opportune fortunes were left invariably at opportune moments." No young sewing room listener "was ever harrowed too long or allowed to rust her crochet needles *entirely* with tears."[4]

Burnett's vivid imagination often worked upon life as it worked in art. Apples and jugs of water added a festive air to the children's story sessions, but when apples were no longer available someone substituted raw turnips. Frances refused to admit to the others or to herself that the turnips tasted "nasty." To do so would be to lose "an atmosphere—an illusion. And she was very fond of her illusions" (0, chap. 8). Burnett would later embrace this label by calling herself publicly "The Romantick Lady,"[5] and her biographers would find her fondness for illusions and happy endings a central theme of her life and fiction. In the preface to his biography of his mother, *The Romantick Lady,* Vivian Burnett playfully gives credence to her claim made especially to children that she was a fairy with magic power to bring about happy endings. Similarly, Vivian's wife, Constance Buel Burnett, titled her biography of Burnett for children *Happily Ever After.*[6]

Biographer Thwaite is more critical of these personality traits. She suggests that Burnett's imagination often led her to expect far more than reality could give and that she was therefore always *Waiting for the Party,* the title of Thwaite's biography. According to Thwaite, Burnett's imagination made her restless—"the party" was always in another room; and it frequently led her to a dishonest denial of unpleasant realities in her life and fiction—too often, she tried to pretend that turnips were apples.

Wife and Mother, the "Coming Woman" in Fiction

During the decade after she published her first story in 1868, however, Burnett did not deceive herself about the need to work hard if she wanted more apples than turnips in her life. In 1869 the family moved to Knoxville where in 1870 Burnett's mother died. In a letter of the time Burnett says that it is she who will have to raise the family from being "shabby, genteel beggars." She wants more of life's "pretty, graceful things" and "a chance to see the world." She was writing five or six ten- or twelve-dollar stories a month for ladies' magazines, but felt she had to see more of life if she were to grow: "I cannot weave silk if I see nothing but calico—calico—calico."[7]

She did manage to turn the calico of her life in Knoxville into the silken love-story conventions of *Vagabondia,* her first work of long fiction, serialized as *Dolly* in *Peterson's,* in 1873. The carpenters and house painters who sang in the Hodgson parlor became artists in Bohemian London. The spirited Dolly was a self-portrait, and Dolly's faithful lover Griff had a life model in Burnett's childhood sweetheart, Swan Burnett. The son of the doctor in New Market, the small town where the Hodgsons first settled, Swan was now a medical student in New York, and he very much wanted to marry the young woman back in Tennessee. A lover's misunderstanding separates Dolly from Griff before their tearful reunion at the end of Burnett's book. It was the young author's having saved enough money to visit England that made Swan apprehensive in 1872, and so he exacted a promise to marry him upon her return.

On her way to England, Burnett stopped over in New York where she had her first contact with literary people. In 1871 she had broken into the realm of "actual literature" when *Scribner's* accepted "Surly Tim," a Lancashire mining story using considerable dialect. Her New York host was Richard Watson Gilder, the editor with whom she would work during much of a long career publishing with Scribner's. Frances spent fifteen months in England, sending back stories that appeared almost monthly in *Scribner's, Harper's,* and the magazines which bought her stories earlier. In 1873 she returned to marry Swan in New Market, and they took a honeymoon in New York where she met George MacDonald, Bret Harte, and other literary lions.

During the first three years of her marriage Burnett wrote to help support her increasing family. Lionel was born in 1874, and in 1875 an arrangement for Burnett to write for *Peterson's* allowed the family to move to Paris where her husband wanted to study. He was happy, but she, tired from overwork and again pregnant, was frequently depressed. Nevertheless, she finished *That Lass o' Lowrie's,* a novel of Lancashire mining life, serialized in *Scribner's* in 1876, the year Burnett's second and last child, Vivian, was born. Although she was by

now earning a name as a writer, she was apparently trying to make
her role as wife primary, as least socially. Manchester friends the Burnetts visited on their way home found her "like many thousands of
other young English wives and mothers," with "nothing" of the
"typical authoress" about her.[8]

When the Burnetts returned from Europe in 1876 they were in
debt; Frances and the children stayed with her in-laws in New Market while Swan set up practice as an eye specialist in Washington,
D.C. His family joined him in 1877; and the next five years, when
Frances was twenty-eight through thirty-two years old and her sons
were under eight, were among the most productive of her life. In
1877 *That Lass o' Lowrie's* and *Surly Tim and Other Stories* sold well in
England and in America. American reviewers were extravagant
in their praise, claiming that for dramatic power she had no equal,
not even George Eliot.[9] In England, *Punch* paid *Lass* the compliment
of a burlesque, and four persons, including Charles Reade, dramatized the book without consulting Burnett. This was the first of several copyright battles she would face, and her strategy—to dramatize
the book herself—inaugurated a theater career that would include at
least fifteen dramatizations of her fiction and two original play collab-
orations.[10] As would frequently be the case, she helped with rehearsals of this first play, which opened to mixed reviews in New York in
1878. Meanwhile, she was finishing *Haworth's,* a novel of Lancashire
industrial life. Published in 1879, it increased her reputation in England as well as in America, but a Philadelphia reviewer wondered if
this "woman of genius" could not "get out of Lancashire and its dialect and give us an American story."[11]

Burnett did turn to Americans as main characters of the novels and
plays she published during 1880–81. She paid tribute to her own
youth in rural Tennessee through her sympathetic portrayal of a
farmer's daughter in *Louisiana* (1880). A young woman from Nevada
charms her relatives in a staid English village in *A Fair Barbarian*
(1881), which some readers saw as a lighthearted answer to Henry
James's *Daisy Miller* (1878). Burnett admired James greatly; they
would become friends in the 1890s when both had plays on the London boards and lived in neighboring country houses in southern England; and the international themes of Burnett's later fiction invite
comparison with James. For now, however, Burnett's admiration of
James was matched by his anonymous, unfavorable review of *Young
Folk's Ways,* the 1883 London version of *Esmeralda,* which in 1881

had opened a successful run in New York. This, Burnett's second play, was based on an earlier story about rural, newly rich Americans in Paris. The last and most complex novel Burnett wrote during this fruitful period of her career was American in milieu as well as characters. Serialized in 1881, *Through One Administration* dramatized the political and social intrigue of contemporary life in the nation's capital. Focusing on a woman who is celebrated for her social gaiety but unhappy in her marriage, this realist novel has one of the few unhappy endings in Burnett's fiction.

Through One Administration is based on Burnett's observations during three years of living in Washington, D.C. Soon after they arrived, the Burnetts were pulled near the center of the city's social life. Swan's ophthalmology practice grew, and he became a published lecturer and professor at Georgetown University. A neighbor and family friend, James Garfield, became president in 1880, and during his brief tenure the Burnett boys often played in the White House. As a successful novelist, of course, Burnett herself was soon a welcome guest in most social circles, and she was receiving attention outside the capital as well. In 1879 she was feted by the Boston Papyrus Club, where she met Louisa May Alcott and Mary Mapes Dodge, editor of *St. Nicholas*. She visited Emerson at Concord and the Dickinsons in Amherst. During the summer of 1880, she was at Nook Farm to collaborate with William Gillette on the stage version of "Esmeralda." Also there that summer were Charles Dudley Warner and Harriet Beecher Stowe, whose *Uncle Tom's Cabin* Burnett had loved as a child. Probably at about this time, she met Mark Twain, who was an admirer of her work; back in Washington, she was delighted to have Oscar Wilde gild her parlor. These associations with well known writers were only to be expected of someone her publisher considered the "Coming Woman" in literature.[12] After *Through One Administration,* Burnett was in fact at the pinnacle of her reputation as far as what she had earlier called "actual literature" was concerned. In 1883, a *Century* article surveying the foremost young American writers included Burnett with William Dean Howells, Henry James, George Washington Cable, and Constance Fenimore Woolson.[13]

Little Lord Fauntleroy and the Ideal Mother

On the surface, at least, Burnett's personal life prospered too. She had two sons she enjoyed, a husband who encouraged her career by managing its business side, and more financial security than she had had since a very young child. Newspaper accounts described her as living "quietly and pleasantly. . . . Although professionally literary, she is so domestic that those unacquainted with her writings would not suspect the fact." Privately, however, there were strains in her marriage and within herself. Swan was unhappy that Frances's career took her away from home so often, and Frances was sometimes deeply depressed. In a fragment apparently written about this time, she lamented that those around her regarded her as only "a kind of pen-driving machine, warranted not to wear out. . . . Write-write-write. Be sick, be tired, be weak and out of ideas, if you choose; but write!"[14]

For three years, from 1882 to 1884, in fact, the "pen-driving machine" did stop; Frances was often ill as well as depressed. In the five years since moving to Washington, she had written four novels, two plays, and many short stories; conscious of her lack of formal education, she had also tried to follow a reading course a friend at the Congressional Library had outlined for her. In addition, while she was meeting these and other demands of her career, she was probably finding it difficult even to approximate the ideals her era had for a wife and mother. There was undoubtedly much of Burnett herself in the unhappily married heroine of *Through One Administration,* who tells a man who adores her: "You have an ideal for everything . . . especially for women. . . . You are always telling yourself that they are good, and pure, and loving, and faithful; that they adore their children, and are true to their friends. It is very pretty, but it is not always the fact. You try to believe it is true of me; but it is not."[15] The fictional Bertha Amory decides to stay with her husband for the sake of the children. Burnett, too, would wait until 1898 to divorce; but from about 1884, she increasingly lived away from home, with friends or in rented homes in Europe as well as America. The boys lived alternately with their father and their mother.

The ideal always had a special hold on Burnett's imagination, as forecast by the happy endings of her childhood stories, her preference of illusory apples to real turnips. If her marriage could not continue "happily ever after," if even the illusion of being the ideal wife was no longer possible, another ideal was still open—that of devoted mother. "The one perfect thing in my life was the childhood of my boys," she would later repeat;[16] now she put that "one perfect thing" into a work of fiction which, as in the stories she told as a child, brought her an "opportune fortune" at an "opportune moment" and abruptly changed the course of her life and fiction. The innocent, beautiful hero of *Little Lord Fauntleroy* was based on Burnett's youngest son, Vivian, who was eight in 1885 when the book was serialized in *St. Nicholas,* a magazine for children. And Fauntleroy's widowed mother was an idealized portrait of Burnett herself, as is clear from her later account of "How Fauntleroy Occurred."[17] Thematically, the book was a continuation of her earlier works showing that American democratic values stand up well in the more class-conscious Europe: A disinherited American boy charms his irascible English grandfather; without corrupting his own innocence or seriously questioning his grandfather's aristocratic values, the child wins back his noble title and fortune. It was a fairy tale calculated to win hearts on both sides of the Atlantic during an era when an increasing number of Americans were able to buy the sophistication which the English often needed to sell. Gladstone told Burnett he believed the book would have great effect in bringing greater understanding and good feeling between the two nations.[18]

Burnett's portrait of an ideal child was bound to be successful also because it rode the crest of a fin de siecle sentimentality about childhood and was to become one of its most notorious examples once the wave had subsided. This notoriety was due as much to the book's phenomenal success as to its own excess. Published as a book in 1886, it soon became a best-seller in English and was translated into over a dozen languages. Burnett's 1888 stage version was popular in England, France, and America, where it ran on Broadway four years and toured the country with road companies almost as numerous as those producing *Uncle Tom's Cabin* and *Ben Hur.* In 1893, *Little Lord Fauntleroy* appeared in more American libraries than any book except *Ben Hur,*[19] and the book's popularity spawned a variety of related products such as Fauntleroy toys, playing cards, writing paper, chocolate, and the notorious dark velvet suits with lace collars, emphasized in Reginald Birch's illustrations for the book. It was this fashion foisted on unwilling children as much as Burnett's story itself that made Little Lord Fauntleroy a by-word for "sissy."

Burnett and her son Vivian, on whom Little Lord Fauntleroy was based, would eventually share this notoriety. For now, however, the book and play based on it brought her financial independence and the opportunity to live out many of the romantic dreams she had had during her youth as a "genteel beggar." In 1887 she took her boys to

England, where they enjoyed the pageantry of Queen Victoria's Jubilee. During the coming years spent mostly in Europe, her celebrity as Fauntleroy's author introduced her socially to royalty, persons of noble title, a prime minister, and a variety of writers, artists, and theater people. While maintaining a large house in Washington, D.C., in which Swan lived until 1895, she rented comfortable apartments and homes in London, rural England, Paris, Florence, and Rome. In addition to enjoying the fashionable social life she had earlier known only through the conventions of magazine fiction, she was now able to act the role of fairy godmother and bring about "happy endings" in the lives of needy relatives and friends.

Her own boys, of course, were frequently recipients of her largesse. She wanted to give them every possible educational and cultural advantage, and often took them with her on her travels. Perhaps to compensate for the times she left them with their father, she gladly supplied money to support their projects such as printing and electrical experiments. In 1890, the illness of fifteen-year-old Lionel especially elicited her penchant for dramatizing in her life her fictional ideals, in this case that of sacrificing mother as well as fairy godmother. When American doctors pronounced Lionel's consumption incurable, she spent almost nine months taking him to various sanatoriums in Europe. Wanting her son to die happy, she created around him the fiction that he was not really very ill but rather a traveling "Prince Imperial" whose every wish was to be granted. When he died, she thanked God for the success with which she had hid her own suffering to play her role: "I never allowed him to know that I was *really* anxious about him . . . that he had consumption or that he was in danger—and when he died he passed away so softly and quickly that I know he wakened in the other world without knowing how he had left this one."[20] In her dead son's name, Burnett subsequently engaged in various projects to help poor and invalid children.

Literature of the Child, a Handsome Doctor, and the Theater

If *Little Lord Fauntleroy* demonstrated to Burnett that she had a writing "gift" which could make her "life a brilliant, successful thing" she could share with others,[21] the book also changed the course of her literary career. Most of what she published until 1896 was for or about children. In stories such as "Editha's Burglar," "Sara

Crewe," and "Little Saint Elizabeth," she portrayed children who, like Fauntleroy, have a beneficent effect on adults; in 1893 she published her own childhood memoir, *The One I Knew the Best of All.* *Little Lord Fauntleroy* also removed any doubts Burnett may have had about whether to continue writing for the theater. In 1888 E. V. Seebohm put *Little Lord Fauntleroy* on stage in London, and, with her British publisher Warne, Burnett rushed into court. Burnett eventually kept her "dear little boy" from being spoiled by others,[22] but only through a legal technicality. In an era when authors felt their rights were being insufficiently protected by existing laws, Burnett's victory won her greater fame; the British Society of Authors used an inscribed diamond bracelet to express their gratitude for the precedent established by her case. Four days after the judgment against Seebohm, Burnett opened *The Real Little Lord Fauntleroy* in London, and the *Times* declared it "in all respects superior to the pirated version." The London success was repeated in New York and Boston, where it had eighty-year-old Oliver Wendell Holmes and his theater party "all crying like babies."[23]

Burnett's next play, *Phyllis* (London, 1889), a domestic drama based on *The Fortunes of Philippa Fairfax* (1888), was a critical failure. One critic told her to keep writing stories but let experienced dramatists adapt them for her. By this time, however, Burnett had personal as well as professional incentives for continuing her theater career. She had become the champion of a young London doctor who wanted to move from amateur dramatic productions into the professional theater. The scion of a clerical family that had interdicted his theatrical aspirations earlier, Stephen Townesend was just the person to elicit Burnett's penchant for becoming benefactress. In addition, she felt indebted to him for his faithful medical services and moral support during the months in 1890 when she was seeking a cure for her dying son. Burnett made Townesend her business manager and solicited his help in dramatizing "Editha's Burglar," which played London in 1890 as *Nixie.* They collaborated on *The Showman's Daughter,* a play about the proprietor of a waxworks show who educates his daughter as a lady; producer Burnett gave Townesend the lead role. A week after the play opened in 1892, however, the death of a popular member of the royal family put the country into mourning, and the lack of theatergoers forced the play to close with a deficit.

Burnett collaborated with Constance Fletcher in writing her next play, *The First Gentleman of Europe,* but she had Townesend follow her to New York to help with the rehearsals for its production in 1897. The reviews were less than enthusiastic, but before the play finished its run, Townesend was helping her answer theater managers' requests for a stage adaptation of her best-seller, *A Lady of Quality* (1896). Townesend was given an acting part in its American production, and once again their teamwork encountered bad luck. During its 1897 opening in Detroit, the theater, with the production's sets and costumes, burned to the ground. Burnett disliked its resurrected production in New York, and the play was not well reviewed by the critics there, in Boston, or London.

Clearly, Burnett could claim only a mixed success for her theatrical career in the decade after *Little Lord Fauntleroy* became an international best-seller. The critics were on the whole indifferent to her plays, but her moderate success with audiences gave her a safe platform from which she could commiserate with her friend Henry James, who was at the same time being booed back to his novelist's study for good. Burnett's personal life was a similar mixture of success, happiness, and pain during this era. In London, she continued a rich social life, and she brought her favorite sister Edith and Edith's son to England. Burnett's expanding household also included her personal doctor, business manager, and theatrical protégé Stephen Townesend, who at some point probably became her lover as well.

The high but frustrated aspirations which made Townesend appealing to Burnett's romantic imagination, however, also made him temperamental and sometimes hard to live with. Too often also, bouts of ill health made difficult her continual work to support her increasingly expensive life-style. Her earlier tendency toward invalidism was abetted by a brain concussion she suffered in an 1889 cart accident. Afraid that her writing abilities might have been impaired, she was deeply depressed during her long convalescence. While regaining consciousness after the fall, she moaned fears that there was something her boys wanted which she could not give them. She was probably nagged by guilt because of her decision to leave them with their father while she pursued her own career, and she observed a long period of mourning after Lionel's death in 1890.

Burnett's private sorrows were compounded by unfavorable reports about her personality and life-style. Many of these stemmed from public curiosity about the mother and sons at the center of the Fauntleroy phenomenon. To combat rumors that she fantastically dressed and posed her boys to impress strangers, for example, Burnett averred in print that her "taste for the picturesque" had not led her "to transform two strong, manly robust boys into affected, abnormally self-conscious, little mountebanks."[24] Eventually she became wary of the press which repaid her with more articles berating her for superficial conversation, a failed or unconventional marriage. Reporters plagued her about the possibility of another Fauntleroy, and critics increasingly expressed dismay at the direction her writing had taken. In 1889, the *Literary News* regretted that she "now longs more to impress upon the world her personal magnetism, brilliant conversational talents and fascinating 'woman's way', than to retire from publicity, work hard, study and acquire fresh, unused material which she might put into a work that would live after her pretty reddish-brown hair is white and all her original and often outré costumes have . . . worn out." By 1892 another critic worried that an "over-great fertility" was leading her toward "gush and verbal redundancy." Repeatedly, critics wondered when she would fulfill the promise she had shown in *That Lass o' Lowrie's* and *Through One Administration.*[25]

Parting Company with the Critics

Burnett answered these pleas with *A Lady of Quality* (1896), about a strong-willed girl reared as a boy, who later accidentally kills her former lover, hides his body, and lives happily without punishment or regrets. The Scribner's editor considered Burnett's manuscript "tawdry" and "artificial," but he thought it might also become "popular." The novel did sell well in both England and America and on the whole critics agreed with the editor's estimate of its literary value. Burnett had to defend the "bad language" of her "unprincipled" heroine as well as the fictional portrayal of "topics that are not savory."[26] In subject matter and tone, *A Lady of Quality* was a drastic departure from her previous best-seller, *Little Lord Fauntleroy*. It did not mark a change in Burnett's willingness to make the most of a popular thing, however; she quickly revised it for the stage and wrote *His Grace of Osmonde* to comply with Scribner's request for a companion volume to be in bookstores when the play opened in 1897.

A Lady of Quality widened the split between critical opinion and popular appeal that characterized the rest of Burnett's writing career. Critics apparently took the novel as a signal that Burnett no longer sought nor could merit serious attention. In 1899, *In Connection with The De Willoughby Claim* contained some of the local color realism for which Burnett had earlier been praised, but many critics now ignored her effort.[27] It is probable that Burnett exaggerated when she said she never read her critics. It is also likely, however, that after the press panned or ignored the three novels she published during the last five years of the century, she decided to please not the critics but the large audience she could be fairly sure was always there for her work. In less than two weeks she dashed off for the *Century* and *Cornhill, The Making of a Marchioness* (1901), a Cinderella tale set in fashionable British society; she then obliged her publisher's request for a sequel with *The Methods of Lady Walderhurst* (1901).

During the last years of the century, Burnett also apparently decided to stop trying to please the critics of her life. In 1898 she legalized her domestic arrangement by divorcing Swan. The press noted that the proceedings were by "mutual consent" and speculated that "while Mrs Burnett never posed as a new woman," her "very advanced ideas as to the rights of women and the duties of a wife, which in no way accord with those of her husband," were the origin of the split. Soon, however, that explanation was too tame: Burnett's business and stage manager Stephen Townesend was named the cause of domestic friction, and she had to deny rumors that they would marry. In fact, the rift between the Burnetts had predated her acquaintance with Townesend, but in February 1900 she did take the step allowing a New York newspaper to headline the "AMAZING MARRIAGE OF . . . AMERICA'S GREAT WOMAN NOVELIST, TO HER PRIVATE SECRETARY."[28]

The marriage was considered "amazing" in part because of the difference in their ages. While Townesend was not "YOUNG ENOUGH TO BE HER SON," as the headline announced, he was, at age forty, ten years her junior. The marriage might have been considered "amazing" also because Burnett had apparently stated publicly that matrimony hindered a person's devotion to art. Ann Thwaite, Burnett's biographer, maintains that there is some mystery about why the marriage took place, for the marriage soured immediately, and Burnett should not have been surprised; during their tension-filled relationship of over ten years, she had not blinded herself to Townesend's volatile temperament. Since Burnett had "no illusions" about Townesend, Thwaite comes to the "reluctant conclusion" that he "literally blackmailed" her into marrying him to gain freer access to her money. As partial evidence Thwaite offers a letter Burnett wrote to Edith in May 1900, just two months after the wedding: "He talks about my 'duties as a wife' as if I had married him of my own accord—as if I had not been forced and blackguarded and blackmailed into it." Thwaite speculates that Townesend threatened to ruin her with revelations about their relationship in the early 1890s. "But for the fact that he could not injure me quite as much unmarried as married," Burnett continued in her letter to Edith, "I should never have got the divorce [from Burnett]. His [Townesend's] most infamous threat, you know, used to be that he would get Dr. Burnett to join him in hounding me down."[29]

The motives Burnett and Townesend had for marrying may never be precisely determined, but it is certain that with a few exceptional interludes the marriage was not a happy one. Vivian would not visit his mother when Townesend was with her, and the newly married couple were often apart. In 1902, domestic tensions, overwork, and neuritis sent Burnett to a New York sanatorium for a rest; when Townesend visited her, she told him she would no longer live with him. The two lived separate lives until he died of pneumonia and exhaustion at age fifty-five, in 1914.

Donning Roles, the Life and Fiction of Romance

Marital discord and unfavorable comments by her critics often made Burnett's life difficult, but royalties from her books allowed her to find refuge in Maytham Hall, a country estate in Kent she leased from 1898 through 1907. The commodious house allowed her to entertain whom and when she liked; on the ample grounds she became a passionate gardener, a role which gave her solace the rest of her life. Maytham also provided a romantic setting for Burnett the famous writer: In white dress and large hat she would sit in her favorite rose garden to write. And, with its neighboring village Rolvenden, Maytham allowed Burnett to add lady of the manor to her repertoire of dramatic roles. She was delighted to find that "there is a nice old square-towered church at Rolvenden with a Maytham pew for the gentry at the Hall and a Maytham pew for the servants." "I shall have school 'treats' in the Park," she promised. "When I drive through the village, people touch their hats and I know almost everyone is related to me by baker-age or brewer-age or blacksmith-age. Just you give me time to make them adore me." They did adore her. In 1971, over sixty years after Burnett had left Maytham, Ann Thwaite found Rolvenden residents still telling stories of Burnett's kindness; a plaque in the church reminded visitors that she had been "careful to maintain good works."[30]

Maytham Hall made Burnett realize that she wanted a home and a garden of her own. In 1909 she moved into an Italianate villa she built in Plandome, Long Island, New York. She had become an American citizen in 1905—to avoid her British husband's claims on her property, Thwaite suggests—and until she died in 1924, she considered the Plandome mansion her home, though she often spent winters in a house she bought in Bermuda. Burnett often shared her homes with her sister Edith as well as Vivian and his family. In 1914 Burnett gave Vivian and his bride a four-month honeymoon cruise around the world, and the couple thanked her with two girls born in 1916 and 1918. Burnett now named herself "Fairy Grandmother" and predicted that "The Fairy Godmother will pale by comparison."[31]

Burnett's delight in her grandchildren during her final years was only a more personal version of a lifelong enjoyment of children. She usually included several children among her special friends and was often at her best with children rather than adults. At a party in Washington, D.C., for example, the young author's reserve disappointed a hostess who wanted to show her off; when some children in the room elicited from Burnett a story, however, "her face, her whole figure" became "radiant" with emotions also "reflected in the small faces about her."[32] Children often participated more wholeheartedly than adults when Burnett wanted to play Fairy Godmother. Once, when she waved her lorgnette and produced a toy boat she had discovered a young friend wanted, the boy was so impressed by her "magic" that he asked not for the boat but the lorgnette, "the thing that gets the things." Burnett liked to act out stories with children, informally or in amateur theatricals. *"Le bon Dieu* so made me that I can 'be' any number of persons at a moment's notice," she observed.[33] Adults might find affectation, conceit, or even sadness in the romantic roles and fancy clothes Burnett loved, but children apparently saw her otherwise. At the turn of the century, eight-year-old Pamela Maude and her sister often visited Burnett at Maytham; seventy years later, in a letter to Thwaite, Maude defended Burnett: "When we stepped into the Fairy Tree and she read us *Sara Crewe,* she seemed to be completely forgetful of *herself."* Burnett "was not 'bogus', not vulgar." "She saw things in the same way as ourselves."[34]

At about the same time that Burnett was reading *Sara Crewe* to little Pamela Maude at Maytham, rehearsals were underway in London for a stage version of the story. As *A Little Unfairy Princess* and *A Little Princess,* the play opened in London in December 1902 and in New York the next month. The play was declared a worthy successor to *Little Lord Fauntleroy,* and in 1905 Burnett published *A Little Princess,* a book expanding the earlier *Sara Crewe* to include new material from the play. During the next decade Burnett produced some of her best writing for children, notably *The Secret Garden* (1911), but also the often effective adventure romance *The Lost Prince* (1915); in 1912 she turned a children's story, "Racketty-Packetty House," into a play for the Children's Theater in New York. Children figure prominently in two other short books written during this period, *In The Closed Room* (1905) and *The White People* (1917). In both, the ghosts of dead children appear to those who love them. These stories grew out of the faith in an afterlife which gave Burnett solace after her son Lionel died, though she was neither conventionally religious nor much impressed by the seances or psychic research of the time. The quick conversion of a man intent on suicide in *The Dawn of a To-morrow* (1906) caused its stage version (1909) to be called a "tribute to the New Thought—the cults of the Faith Cure, Mind Cure, Rest Cure or the theology of Mrs. Eddy,"[35] and some readers saw the effect of Christian Science in *The Secret Garden.* During her many and varied illnesses, Burnett had in fact become convinced that the mind has great power over the body's health, but she denied any association with specific religious movements of the day.

The Dawn of To-morrow joined *A Little Princess* as the more successful of Burnett's excursions into the theater during the last twenty-five years of her life. Neither *The Pretty Sister of José* (1903) nor *That Man and I* (1904; an adaptation of *In Connection with The De Willoughby Claim*) scored well with audiences or critics. According to Thwaite, Burnett wrote plays from *The Making of a Marchioness* (called *Glenpeffer*) and two other books of the period, *The Shuttle* and *T. Tembarom;* in 1904 she completed *Judy O'Hara,* about a female Robin Hood dressed in white. None of these plays saw production.[36]

During the last twenty-five years of her life Burnett found the greatest audience success with her four long romances. *The Shuttle* (1907), about Anglo-American social relationships, sold so well that it entirely paid for the lavish home she built in Plandome. In *T. Tembarom* (1913), she took a favorite character from *The Shuttle* and created an adult version of the Fauntleroy rags-to-riches tale. In *The Head of the House of Coombe* and *Robin* (1922), she set her romances in an England being changed by world war. Reactions to these popular romances indicate the decline in critical respect for her work which marked the final era of her life. In 1907 and 1913, critics could be patronizing. *The Boston Transcript,* for example, called *T. Tembarom* "an old-fashioned tale that is sometimes romantic, sometimes realistic, sometimes plausible, sometimes incredible but always enjoyable." By 1922, however, critics let Burnett know that her day was over. The *Boston Transcript* still admitted that even when "not in her best mood" Burnett "is far better than the average storyteller of the day." More typical were critics who claimed that "lush sentiments flow from her pen with a sweetness that suggests syrup rather than plain ink" and that *Robin* was "the apotheosis of Burnettian slush."[37]

Back home at Plandome, with her garden, grandchildren, and guests, Burnett was probably not much surprised or hurt by these final barbs from the critics. During the war, she had corresponded with soldiers who had enjoyed her work. One told her that he "should like to receive three such books" as *T. Tembarom* "every week. . . . I hope it has done dozens of gloomy beggars as much good as it did me."[38] Expressions such as this from her readers and the continuing sales of her books must have meant much to an author who during her final illness told her son, "With the best that was in me I have tried to write more happiness into the world."[39] She died at home in Plandome on 29 October 1924.

Chapter Two

From Magazine Fiction to Romance to Realist Novel (1868–84)

Between 1868 and 1884 Burnett wrote many short stories and six longer works of fiction. She began the period at age nineteen seeing herself as a producer of enough "pot boilers" to help support herself and her family; by the end of the period at age thirty-five she had won a foothold in what she called "the world of actual literature,"[1] for critics now compared her favorably to major writers in both England and America. In much of her short fiction as well as in three short romances, *Dolly* (1873) retitled *Vagabondia* (1883), *Louisiana* (1880), and *A Fair Barbarian* (1881), Burnett moved from self-conscious dependence to graceful facility in the use of the conventions of ladies' magazine fiction. And with notable but uneven success she followed more sophisticated models such as Elizabeth Gaskell and Henry James in her realist novels, *That Lass o' Lowrie's* (1877), *Haworth's* (1879), and *Through One Administration* (1883).

Early Short Fiction

Most of Burnett's early magazine fiction to be discussed appeared in five collections published during the years when *That Lass o' Lowrie's* and *Haworth's* were winning her critical recognition in England and America: *Surly Tim and Other Stories* (1877), *Earlier Stories* (1878), *Our Neighbor Opposite* (1878), *A Quiet Life and The Tide on the Moaning Bar* (1878), and *Natalie and Other Stories* (1879). Some of these stories indicate that the young, largely self-educated author had considerable narrative gifts, and many show her apprenticeship use of character types, plot formulas, scenes, and themes she would use later in her more famous fiction for children and adults.

Burnett wrote a considerable number of love stories using the popular Cinderella formula—an attractive young woman wins the affec-

tion of a man whose sophistication, wealth, or social class is superior
to hers. Suspense is created by the question of whether the lovers will
overcome obstacles such as social class, rivals, and misunderstand-
ings. Examples include the first two stories she published, in *Godey's
Lady's Book,* in 1868—"Miss Carruthers' Engagement" and "Hearts
and Diamonds"—as well as a considerable number in *Earlier Stories,*
which first appeared in *Peterson's Ladies' Magazine.* In one of these,
"Lindsay's Luck," Burnett varies the formula by having a male protagonist, the son of an American tradesman who wins the affection of
a haughty English lady of title. Later, Burnett would make yet another adaptation of this Cinderella formula by turning the young
American lover into an American boy who courts his haughty English
grandfather, in *Little Lord Fauntleroy;* the winsome child hero of this
best-seller would also share many personality traits with the protagonists of her early love stories—an innocent love of fun, earnest sympathy for others, and lack of self-consciousness.

In a second group of love stories, Burnett shows female protagonists learning to fulfill social expectations for a woman, especially a
wife and mother. In "Miss Crespigny," "Kathleen Mavourneen,"[2] "La
Monsieur de la Petite D'ame,"[3] and "Natalie: A Story of the Latin
Quarter,"[4] for example, Burnett's belles must reject the shallowness,
selfishness, and sometimes cynicism of their youthful coquetry to
learn the serious sympathy for others expected of a good woman.
Usually, this transformation comes about through the educative example of a virtuous, domestic woman or through the patient love of
a male admirer or a husband. As is typical of much popular fiction,
these stories sometimes apparently question traditional ideals, through
their heroines' early rebellion, but the ideals are reaffirmed by the end
of the story, since the heroines eventually accept the expected female
roles.

One story in this category is interesting, however, because the
eventual affirmation of the traditional ideal, here female domesticity,
does not seem convincing because of the depth of the questioning
that preceded it. In "The Woman Who Saved Me,"[5] a married
woman from London has lost her first child, is convinced her husband
does not love her, suffers from a vague but serious illness, and visits
her happily domestic female friend in a town by the sea. Untypically,
Burnett uses first-person narration and effectively evokes in the voice
of the protagonist someone who is possibly hypochondriacal, certainly

self-absorbed, self-pitying, listless, and bored. Burnett creates suspense by making the reader wonder about the cause of the woman's malaise. Parts of the story seem a forecast of Kate Chopin's *The Awakening* (1899)—the woman's early protestations that she does not love her husband, does not particularly like children, never loved her baby who died; and her seaside flirtation with another man. But Burnett does not explore the woman's dissatisfactions and their implications as fully as does Chopin; instead she resorts to familiar conventions, however unconvincing in this case, to explain the woman's malaise and bring about its cure—the woman had misunderstood her husband, who really does love her; and her friend "saves" her by providing the model of marital fidelity she will henceforth follow. In the protagonist of this story, it is not difficult to see Burnett's own depression, illness, and marital dissatisfaction, which she would explore more fully later in *Through One Administration*.

A third group of Burnett's early love stories portrays the dark side of the convention of romantic attachments across class lines. Most of these, for example, "Smethurstes,"[6] "A Quiet Life," "The Tide on the Moaning Bar," and "Mére Giraud's Little Daughter,"[7] rehearse sentimentally the familiar story of the pretty lower-class woman who is ruined by a thoughtless aristocrat and then dies, by disease or suicide. "Jarl's Daughter" is by far the most effective in this group largely because this story of a fisherman's daughter ruined by a dashing captain is told by another woman. The resulting distance and economy of narration almost allow the usually pathetic fallen woman to become a tragic heroine. As Burnett's "Cleo" strides to the sea to commit suicide as did her famous Egyptian namesake, she holds her "statuesque head erect" like "some savage queen."[8]

Proud Cleo in "Jarl's Daughter" exemplifies a character type that recurs in Burnett's fiction of this period: a Junoesque, independent, frequently sharp-tongued young woman from the working classes. She occurs several times in a fourth set of stories that can be grouped not so much by specific plot formulas or character types but by the attempt to portray working-class life in provincial England and America. The stories set in America and the later *Louisiana* participated in the movement of local color realism in American literature of the time; the stories set in England as well as *That Lass o' Lowrie's* and *Haworth's* were influenced by the social and political novels written in the 1840s and 1850s by Elizabeth Gaskell, Charlotte Brontë,

Benjamin Disraeli, and Charles Dickens. Much of Burnett's fiction in this category uses dialects Burnett had learned during her youth in Lancashire and Tennessee.

"One Day at Arle,"[9] set in a fishing village on the northwest coast of England, shows that Burnett's working-class Juno makes a faithful if difficult wife. In "The Fire at Grantley Mills"[10] and "Surly Tim," Burnett portrays the Lancashire millworkers she had seen as a child in Manchester and Elizabeth Gaskell had portrayed in *Mary Barton* (1848). With his marital problems, sense of social injustice, and violent death in an industrially related accident, the title character in "Surly Tim" is obviously derived from Stephen Blackpool in Dickens's *Hard Times* (1854).

Though set in east Tennessee, "Seth"[11] depicts immigrants from Lancashire who have followed a British-based mining company. In this story, Burnett's exploration of sexual identity and roles takes a turn less conventional than in most of her stories: A homely young Lancashire woman dresses as a man in order to work in the mines managed by a gentleman who had been kind to her in England. When she dies of cholera her secret is guarded by a coarse miner's daughter whom the community had considered her lover. Burnett would later use cross-dressing to explore female identity in *A Lady of Quality*, the heroine of which is dressed and reared as a boy until she is fifteen. In addition, much of *Little Lord Fauntleroy*'s notoriety would be caused by his curls and fancy clothes, which many thought more appropriate for a girl; during Burnett's lifetime, Fauntleroy was played on the stage as often by girls as by boys.

Stories showing the influence of American local color realism include "Lodusky," set in rural North Carolina, and "Esmeralda," in which the daughter of a suddenly rich American farmer is taken to Paris by her ambitious mother.[12] Especially in the stage version of this story Burnett wrote with the help of William Gillette, Esmeralda's father owes much to the wise yokel of Mark Twain, A. B. Longstreet, and other American local color humorists.

For the most part, Burnett's portrayal of regional life and dialect in this group of stories is handled with discipline and authenticity; and she shows a sensitivity to the hardships and cultural deprivations of poverty. In the final analysis, however, she seemed more interested in finding new and appealing settings for her formulaic plots and her development of female character types than in offering a broader social critique. Most stories contain sympathetic portrayals of privileged or sophisticated individuals, and events are often observed from their points of view. In her American stories, she focused on the theme Henry James was then writing about and she herself would explore in much of her own later work—the encounter of a simpler with a more sophisticated culture, regional America with the urban northeast, and especially America with Europe. Taken as a whole, Burnett's early short fiction demonstrates that by the late seventies, when she was beginning to be noticed in America and England as a serious young talent, she had considerable facility in her craft and had charted out much of the territory she would explore more fully later.

Vagabondia

Burnett's first long work of fiction appeared as *Dolly* in *Peterson's* in 1873; in 1883 she published an edited version, giving it the title she preferred, *Vagabondia*.[13] As might be expected, this popular romance elaborates plot formulas and character types from her short fiction. Its love story involves two social sets: the "Bohemians," a household of young artistic aspirants in Bloomsbury; and the "Philistines," an assortment of wealthy aristocrats, most of whom are unimaginative and self-righteous. Burnett's protagonist, Dolly, is a female David who takes her slingshot full of charms into the "camps" of the Philistine warriors (chap. 3), slays the social Goliaths, and returns with patrons for her painter brother and a husband for her younger sister. The romance relies too heavily on melodramatic conventions and needed more vigorous editing—it runs to almost four hundred pages. It has "considerable originality," however, as a *Nation* reviewer in 1878 put it, "in the fact that the heroine, who is a coquette, is also warm-hearted and faithful to her [Bohemian] lover; this is much more interesting than the ordinary superficial view of the case, which makes such heroines throw over a poor young man to take up with a richer one."[14]

Dolly deviates from convention also in not being a beauty. Though she knows how to dress attractively, her primary charms are social, a winsome manner derived from her desire that everyone like her. In this sense, like some of the other coquettes in Burnett's early fiction, Dolly anticipates Little Lord Fauntleroy. She flirts, but she does so openly and motivated by an excess of spirit rather than a desire to collect suitors. She derives her morality from a fairy-tale innocence, believing that if you are good you will be happy. And she has the "romantic" view that lovers are divinely destined for one another. The portrait of Dolly is enhanced by the fact that the young author has achieved sufficient distance on her developing type to comment on it. The narrator is gently skeptical of Dolly's view of love, for example. When Dolly's ingenue sister soon forgets her first, unworthy lover for a better one, the narrator comments, "And why not, my reader? If one rose is not for us, the sun shines on many another as sweet and quite as fair" (chap. 17). Moreover, the narrator describes Dolly's desire that everyone like her as a "weakness" rather than a strength (chap. 8). It is a "weakness," perhaps, because it signals her chief vanity, one not so common in the coquette. In Dolly, the more conventional enjoyment of power over suitors is replaced by a desire to be a power in the lives of everyone; her suitor, whom she quite justifiably treats as a child or a puppy, is simply included in this number. Her greatest satisfaction comes from acting as "the feminine head of the family" (chap. 3)—bringing in money from her jobs as teacher and lady's companion, keeping up the family's spirits, aiding in their individual fortunes.

According to Burnett's son, Vivian, Dolly's personality and aspirations are much like those of its young author at that time.[15] She similarly felt responsible for improving the lot of herself and her siblings in Knoxville, while remaining loyal to her childhood sweetheart, Swan Burnett. This biographical basis may account for some of the "naturalness" the *Nation* reviewer observed in the book, a naturalness he conjectured "many readers" might feel "fairly outweighs the excellent aim but somewhat stilted execution of the more renowned novel," *That Lass o' Lowrie's*.[16]

That Lass o' Lowrie's

That Lass o' Lowrie's, serialized in *Scribner's* in 1876, and published as a book in England and America in 1877, was indeed "more renowned" than *Vagabondia* and deserved to be. In complexity, structure, and economy, this first of Burnett's realist novels represents a vast improvement over the earlier romance. The chief weaknesses of *That Lass o' Lowrie's* lie in its love stories, based on formulas Burnett had often used before: love overcoming barriers of class, misunderstanding, supposed rivals; and a pretty working-class woman ruined by a privileged-class lover. Burnett's readiness to let these conventions do her work for her suggests the validity of her later comment while writing *Through One Administration:* "I hate and detest love stories but it seems that you must have their grinning sentimental skeletons to hang your respectable humanity and drapery upon."[17] Indeed as Ann Thwaite has observed "many of the most strongly loving relationships" in Burnett's fiction are not sexual but rather those "between mother and son, father and daughter, between sisters, between friends."[18] Similarly, it was not those "grinning sentimental skeletons," the love stories, that most successfully engaged Burnett's imagination in *That Lass o' Lowrie's,* but rather the "humanity" she was able to drape upon them, specifically, the life of Lancashire coal miners and their relationships to the company owners and managers, the clergy, the gentry; and the roles of women and female friendship.

At the center of *That Lass o' Lowrie's* is a pit girl, Joan Lowrie, the most fully developed of Burnett's working-class Junos. In her 1893 memoir Burnett claims that Joan, and presumably the other fictional examples of her type, originated in a large, mill-worker's daughter she had observed during her childhood in Manchester. Because of her stature and proud manner, the girl seemed set apart from the friends with whom she occasionally strolled through the square where Burnett lived. Ten-year-old Frances was awed by the girl's goddesslike beauty and self-possession in the face of the threats of her father, who one day came to bully her back home.[19] The importance of this childhood impression is undeniable, but fiction and fact were often inextricably mixed in Burnett's perception of herself and her work—her later claim that Little Lord Fauntleroy was based on her own son Vivian, without acknowledging his obvious progenitors in her fiction, makes that point clear. Similarly, it is possible that Burnett's goddesses in incongruous surroundings owed something to Charles Reade's statuesque women, such as the fisherwoman in his *Christie Johnstone* (1853); Reade seemed to recognize a familiar type, at least, when he dramatized *That Lass o' Lowrie's* in England, without Burnett's permission.

At the beginning of the novel, Joan is an androgynous figure. In part, this is a mark of her class, for the women who worked at the mouth of the mine "wore dress more than half masculine, . . . talked loudly and laughed discordantly."[20] In addition, however, she defies the female roles accepted within her class. She makes it clear she will have no "sweeteartin'," for example. Receiving physical and psychological abuse from her father and being aware of the frequent insensitivity of other men, Joan declares, "I amna ower fond o' men folk

at no time" (2). The novel dramatizes her gradual acceptance of expected female roles, in part because she falls in love with the gentleman engineer of the mines, but, more convincingly, because she is
softened by her protective friendship with the slight, pretty Liz and
Liz's illegitimate child, both outcasts in the community.

In subtlety and honesty, Burnett's portrayal of Liz equals or exceeds that of Joan. To elicit sympathy or to suggest reform in society's treatment of fallen women, novelists had usually idealized their
fictional examples and showed their remorse, as did Gaskell in *Ruth*
(1853); or, they had portrayed such women seeking the desperate
remedies of suicide or infanticide, as did George Eliot in *Adam Bede*
(1859). The personality of Burnett's seduced and abandoned child-
woman may owe something to kittenish Hetty Sorrel in *Adam Bede*,
but Burnett proved herself independent of even this model. Too
"shallow" for remorse, too "characterless" for the dramatic escapes of
suicide or infanticide (135, 34), Liz bears the child only to resent it,
treat it carelessly, and then leave it with Joan when her former lover
beckons again with the promise of pretty ribbons. Only in the death
of "poor Liz" (34) at the door of Joan's abandoned cottage, does Burnett lapse into the more usual melodrama.

The relationship between Joan and Liz is the most sensitively portrayed in the novel. When they first appear together, Joan is defend-
ing Liz from a knot of hostile women. "Seventeen year owd, Liz is,
an' th' world's gone wrong wi' her," Joan says. "I wunnot say as th'
world's gone ower reet wi' ony on us; but them on us as has had th'
strength to howd up agen it, need na set our foot on them as has
gone down" (24). Joan takes Liz and her child to live with her; and,
though she is baffled by Liz's lack of will, her carelessness about past
and future, Joan treats her with affection and a protectiveness un-
touched by condescension. When Liz proves an inept and finally neg-
ligent mother, Joan cares for the child without recrimination. Less
fully developed but still significant is the friendship which grows between Joan and the rector's daughter, Anice Barholm. This charitable
young lady is "too Sunday schooly,"[21] as Burnett admitted, but the
sensitive manner in which Anice encourages Joan's desire to get an
education and create a new identity represents a fairly commendable
attempt to portray female friendship across class lines.

Understandably, class is a more formidable barrier between Joan
and the young mine engineer, Fergus Derrick. Both resist their romantic involvement. Joan accepts Fergus's help when she is bleeding

from her father's blows and fears going home; she endangers her life to prevent her father from harming Fergus; and she goes down into the mines after an explosion to help rescue him. However, she is convinced that she could never be an appropriate wife for him, and resists his personal overtures and leaves town when she is sure that he loves her. For his part, Fergus agonizes over his division between love and his class background; he feels a coward when he turns his decision over to others—he will resign and leave town if the mine owners reject his proposal for mine safety improvements. In the last pages, Joan does accept the proposal of marriage Fergus offers, after he has recovered from his injuries; but she asks him to wait until she has gained the learning and social skills expected of his wife.

Some readers may find this ending unsatisfying, either because Joan's desire to make herself "worthy" (269) of Fergus seems a pathetic betrayal of her earlier class loyalty or because the gulf between the lovers still seems too wide. A scornful statement of the latter response was elicited from the *Nation* reviewer in 1877: "Reading, writing, and ciphering are only a small part of what is needed before this girl could be turned into a civilized being."[22] If the ending of the novel is unconvincing, however, it is primarily because Burnett portrays, and then briefly, only the most dramatic encounters between the lovers; missing are the scenes of less consequential but revealing interaction which make the affection between Joan and Liz so convincing. For Burnett clearly shows an awareness of the barrier which class difference represents, not only through the lovers' resistance to their love but also through the use of symbolic imagery which would mature in her use of a walled garden in her juvenile classic, *The Secret Garden*.

When Joan first visits Anice, she sees her inside the rectory garden. "She's inside o' th' hedge. . . . I'm outside, theer's th' difference," Joan muses. "It a'most looks loike the hedge went aw' around an' she'd been born among th' flowers, and theer's no way out for her—no more than theer's a way in fur me" (48). Similarly, Burnett uses a wall to suggest the class barrier which keeps Joan from Fergus and prevents his pursuing his personal desires. During his illness, he repeatedly envisions Joan coming to him through the narrow mine passage but being stopped by a wall which falls on him and immobilizes him. Through the setting of her last scene, Burnett symbolically suggests that Joan has overcome these hedges and walls. Anice has gotten Joan a position as companion to her grandmother, and it is inside the garden of this woman's house that Fergus finds Joan and she accepts his proposal. In a novel which shows the issues of sex and class to be so intertwined, the ending is likely to elicit an ambiguous response. Viewed one way, Joan's asking for time to make herself "worthy" of her gentleman lover seems like class capitulation; viewed another way, it is sexual defiance and pride. She will come to the marriage as much his equal as possible; she will come when she, not he, is ready, and then not from weakness but from strength.

As the preceding discussion suggests, the social issues in the novel are an integral part of the main plot rather than simply background. The mine explosion, occurring after the company owners reject Fergus's plans for safety improvements, is pivotal in bringing together not only Joan and Fergus but also Burnett's second pair of lovers, Anice Barholm and her father's curate, Paul Grace. Burnett amplifies her social themes also through a variety of other characters. For example, through several contrasting characters she explores the question of what stance the clergy should adopt toward their parishioners, most of whom are skeptical of clerical sincerity or ability to offer genuine help. The rector, Harold Barholm, is self-satisfied, obtuse, and condescending; the shallowness of his pieties is revealed especially in his unsuccessful attempts to bring Liz to an appreciation of her "sin." Barholm is disdainful of his slight, "feminine" (146) curate, whose sensitivity and perseverance finally achieve a success with the miners which was denied to him. And the rector more than meets his match in the town skeptic, Sammy Craddock, whose humorous barroom tirades effectively score against the clergy and the gentry. Unfortunately, Burnett felt she had to provide an antidote to Sammy's impieties through a sentimental portrayal of Joan's encounter with a picture of the suffering Christ that rings false in Joan's character.

In portrayal of minor characters and social themes, *That Lass o' Lowrie's* also suggests the influence of various authors she was trying to emulate in moving beyond the realm of light fiction. Sammy Craddock often sounds like Dickens's Sam Weller, and his role of village pundit is similar to that of Bartle Massey in Eliot's *Adam Bede*. The hard-drinking Dan Lowrie may be derived from a temperance fiction stereotype, but his violence to his daughter and his death resulting from his own villainy are also reminiscent of Bill Sykes in *Oliver Twist*. Similarly, Jud Bates is a Dickensian waif whose wanderings unite the fortunes of characters from different classes. The interrelated love stories and exploration of the clergy's role in labor disputes recalls Charlotte Brontë's *Shirley*. Finally, like Gaskell in *Mary Barton* and Harriet Beecher Stowe in *Uncle Tom's Cabin* (1852)—one of Burnett's childhood favorites—Burnett attempts to show how the socially oppressed view and cope with their lot. Less interested in the documentary value of her novel than were Gaskell and Stowe, however, Burnett rarely includes for their own sake details about the conditions that made the miners' lives wretched. The fact that children worked in the mines, for example, is revealed only through an exclamation of a mother whose ten-year-old son is caught in the mine after the explosion. And Burnett does not seriously question the socioeconomic system itself but rather stresses the human sensitivity and caring needed to alleviate its unfortunate effects. In this respect, it should be remembered, she does not differ from her more famous predecessors in the social and political novel.

When *That Lass o' Lowrie's* came out as a book in 1877, it was reviewed in the *Atlantic Monthly,* where from his editor's chair William Dean Howells was encouraging young American writers and championing the realist movement in fiction. It is therefore not surprising that his reviewer, possibly Thomas Wentworth Higginson, was better able to appreciate the value and promise of the book than his contemporary at the *Nation.* The male characters are "a little too simply conveyed," the *Atlantic* reviewer allowed; but "the three women are drawn with a much more intimate knowledge and sympathy—especially poor 'Liz.' " He found the dialect "admirably managed" and never running "to excess as George MacDonald's Scotch patois does." Finally, he declared that he would not "be surprised to find Mrs. Burnett, in the future, taking a place—not on just the same grounds, but by virtue of merits of her own—with Charlotte Brontë and Mrs. Gaskell."[23]

Haworth's

Being compared favorably to the likes of Brontë, Gaskell, and MacDonald gave Burnett cause for self-congratulation, but it also brought anxiety as she worked on her second realist novel, *Haworth's,* serialized late in 1878 and published as a book in 1879. When she had written *That Lass o' Lowrie's,* she told her editor at Scribner's, she had been "simply writing a story"; now, she was "trying to please the critics." It was "a fatal kind" of "feeling" which she was "trying desperately to overcome."[24] This new novel had a plot which should have engaged the imagination of the young author. After a decade of hard work, she had finally arrived in the "world of actual literature" and had taken residence in the nation's capital; but she was still aware of the deficiencies in her education, was conscious of her roots in less fashionable society, and had reason to worry about what literary success would do to her personal life, especially her marriage. The title character of *Haworth's* is a self-made industrialist in Lancashire who finds his moral and personal life crumbling at the pinnacle of his worldly success. William Dean Howells would write an American version of this story several years later, in *The Rise of Silas Lapham* (1885), though he did not choose to have *Haworth's* reviewed in the *Atlantic Monthly*.

In Howells's defense, *Haworth's* does not measure up to Burnett's achievement in *That Lass o' Lowrie's*. A *Harper's* reviewer in 1879 hit the mark when he said that *Haworth's* demonstrates Burnett's "art as a story-teller,"[25] but is weak in characterization—an evaluation of her relative skill in handling plot and character which would be reiterated later in criticism of her adult works. As in *That Lass o' Lowrie's,* Burnett explores relationships among working, industrial, and aristocratic classes, and she has two sets of lovers whose fates are involved with the affairs of the town company, "Haworth's." In this novel, however, she chose to develop her male rather than female characters, and she focuses on the problems of the business owners, who had remained largely off stage in the previous novel. Congruently, her working-class characters are mainly comic or debased stereotypes and her aristocrats are effete, haughty, and sometimes cowardly. As she placed the center of her sympathy higher on the social ladder, she seemed to be aiming higher on the traditional scale of literary genres. Her portrayal of the proud, capable industrialist, Jem Haworth, ruined by his passion for the aristocratic Rachel Ffrench, suggests that Burnett was reaching for the heights of tragedy. Burnett's second major character is similarly divided between his passion to achieve and his desire to have Rachel. Haworth's engineer, Stephen Murdock, almost allows his love for Rachel to keep him from perfecting the industrial invention which had sapped his father's life.

Burnett's "art as a storyteller" is demonstrated by how she manages her plot to illustrate the operation of the tragic wheel of fortune. At the beginning of the novel, Haworth is near the top of his industrial achievement and Murdock is near the bottom—he is a common laborer for Haworth and is trying to deny his compulsion to work on his father's invention. At the end, Haworth is bankrupt and Murdock's invention is about to make him a wealthy man. In the middle, their developing friendship is ruptured by their love for the same woman. In addition, Haworth's "most tragic of tragedies," "on the very eve of his life's success"[26] is underscored by two other characters who help bring about his ruin. Their cowardice and self-pity are meant to contrast with the pride and nobility Haworth shows when he sets his books in order for his creditors and takes nothing for himself when he leaves town. One of these contrasting characters is the aristocratic dilettante Gerard Ffrench, whom Haworth takes as a partner in an unsuccessful attempt to win favor with his daughter; it is Ffrench's speculations that ultimately cause Haworth's financial ruin. The second character is the worker, Briarley, who for the price of a pint of ale sells his allegiance to strike organizers as well as to Haworth. Ffrench and Briarley both plead that they are only the victims of circumstances, while Haworth acknowledges both traditional causes of the tragic hero's fall, circumstances and his own flaw, his passion.

Burnett proved unable to provide enough "humanity" to flesh out this story, however. There are some effective strokes in her portrayal of Haworth and in his relationship to his engineer, Murdock—Haworth's pain when he realizes his money cannot overcome his crude manners to win Rachel Ffrench's affection, for example, and his attempts to overcome his resentment of Murdock's superior education. But as in *Vagabondia* and *That Lass o' Lowrie's,* Burnett showed herself better able to handle the psychology of work than of love. The behavior resulting from sexual passion in the novel is stilted, conventional, and insufficiently motivated or analyzed.

Burnett is more at home with her Dickensian minor characters. Her portrayal of Haworth's humble mother is sentimental, but better managed is the Briarley household—Briarley's vengeful, will-shaking grandmother; his good-natured but harried wife; and especially their twelve-year-old daughter Janey, who struggles valiantly to keep on her cast-off adult clothes as she cares for her eleven younger siblings and journeys to retrieve her father from the local tavern. Burnett's treatment of the comic Briarley is an index of how her class sympathies have shifted since *That Lass o' Lowrie's.* Like the other malcontents and ineffective workers who make up the labor resistance to Haworth, Briarley is a tool of outside union agitators. No villain like Dan Lowrie in the former book, Briarley is—probably more insulting as a representative of his class—a buffoon. Caught between industry and labor, his thematic role is similar to that of Stephen Blackpool in *Hard Times*. Blackpool's refrain, " 'Tis a muddle," echoes Dickens's own despair at what industrialism has done to the quality of life in Coketown. The more personal message and limited sympathies of Burnett's novel is reflected in Briarley's repeated self-pitying cry, "I'm a misforchnit chap!"

In many ways, Burnett's movement from *That Lass o' Lowrie's* to *Haworth's* parallels that of Gaskell from *Mary Barton* (1848) to *North and South* (1854–55). Both novelists portrayed captains of industry more sympathetically in their second industrial novels as they dramatized businessmen's attempts to be accepted by the traditional aristocracy. In addition, Burnett borrowed plot elements from *North and South* in Rachel Ffrench's personal defiance of a mob of strikers. Unfortunately, Burnett did not imitate Gaskell's growth in character portrayal. In "trying to please the critics" this time, Burnett's literary reach exceeded her ability to grasp.

Louisiana and *A Fair Barbarian*

According to her son, Vivian, "It was a habit of Frances' to slip in a short 'easy' book between big ones, and, in a sense, she did this with the novel [*A Fair Barbarian*] which followed 'Louisiana'—itself, however, hardly a big one."[27] Of the two, *A Fair Barbarian* (1881) is far more clever and graceful; *Louisiana* (1880) is sentimental and leaden, though Burnett probably regarded it as a more serious if not "big" book—in 1881 Scribner's included it with *That Lass o' Lowrie's* and *Haworth's* in a new uniform edition.[28]

In *Louisiana,* Burnett continues a biographically based theme from *Haworth's,* the problem of maintaining an appreciation for one's humble roots after achieving success in a larger social realm. In this case, however, Burnett uses characters and a setting closer to her own experience. Louisiana, the daughter of a wealthy but uncouth farmer in North Carolina, is taken up by a young writer from New York who has come to a nearby resort in search of new material. The latter, a young woman, dresses Louisiana in her own finery and, improbably, succeeds in passing her off to her visiting brother as a young woman from New York. Louisiana eventually resents being used as an amusing experiment, however, and returns to her father who loves her as she is. The story becomes especially sentimental when Louisiana confesses her guilt at being ashamed of him, only to be grieved by his death. The story's ending exemplifies Burnett's penchant in her popular fiction for allowing her main characters to have their cake and eat it too. Louisiana marries the young man from New York, becomes a "book worm" as well as a graceful wearer of stylish clothes, and achieves success as a "new type" among her husband's literary friends in New York;[29] but she also spends her summers in North Carolina, where she keeps a room in her home furnished exactly as it had been when she grew up. This ending may reflect Burnett's own desire to maintain touch with her rural roots now that she was the "Coming Woman" in fiction; for, according to Vivian Burnett, many of the romance's characters were drawn from the kind-hearted people she had known in New Market, Tennessee, the tiny rural town where her family had first settled in America.[30]

A Fair Barbarian, which takes a young American woman to England, is by far the best romance written during this early period of Burnett's career; and it demonstrates that in dramatizing the confrontation between two cultures, she was far more successful in bringing a representative from a simpler culture into a more sophisticated one than in reversing this process, as by having a New York writer come to the rural south, in *Louisiana;* Burnett's satire was more effective when aimed up the social ladder than down. Despite her intention to pay tribute to North Carolina farmers through her portrayal of Louisiana's father, she could not escape condescension; her humor is cheap and makes him appear more pathetic than noble. Perhaps because she admired even the provincial British for their traditions more genuinely than she revered the rural American folks for their morals, she was able to judge the British more severely and at the same time laugh at them with subtler wit.

A Fair Barbarian is set in Slowbridge, a provincial English town whose largely female society is probably based on that in Gaskell's *Cranford* (1853). Octavia Bassett, a young woman from Nevada who comes to visit her maiden aunt in Slowbridge, is Burnett's contribution to the controversy about the American young woman that Henry James had opened with *Daisy Miller* in 1878, and William Dean Howells had continued in *The Lady of the Aroostook* (1879). Octavia affronts the conservative citizens of Slowbridge in almost every way. Her ostentatious clothes and jewels and the frank manner in which she talks about her childhood in "Bloody Gulch" cause the reigning society matron to call her a "barbarian." Her "inscrutably innocent and indifferent air"[31]—she is totally unembarrassed by her inability to play, sing, or speak French—causes the same social arbiter to call her "an impertinent minx" (68). Like the young American women portrayed by James and Howells, Octavia sees no reason for abiding by the social restraints customary for European girls. Like Daisy Miller, she takes a moonlight walk alone with a young man, but unlike Daisy, who gets malaria and dies, Octavia does not suffer because of her freedom. Her good-hearted lack of affectation overcomes Slowbridge's prejudices; a young woman pays her the homage of imitation; and she has a final ace up her sleeve to make her victory complete. She turns down the proposal of Slowbridge's prize bachelor to marry the big, bronzed man who arrives from America.

It is not surprising that some saw Burnett's short romance as an answer to *Daisy Miller,* which was often read as an outrage against American girlhood. In fact, however, Burnett's novel more resembles James's less-famous story, "An International Affair" (1878), in which a young American woman similarly triumphs by turning down the proposal of an English aristocrat. If Burnett was thinking of James as she wrote *A Fair Barbarian,* however, it was not in her main character that she owed her greatest debt—her own fictional gallery, after all, had by now a sufficient number of cheeky charmers. It is most likely that Burnett was trying to imitate James's economy. After reading *The Europeans* in 1878, she had declared that James had a "*neat* imagination." By this she meant "how beautifully he goes all round a thing and what excellent order he leaves it in—with no ends straggling—no gaps—no thin places."[32] Especially if one compares *A Fair Barbarian* with *Vagabondia*—her first attempt to extend the conventions of magazine fiction to novel length—it is clear that this lesson of the master was not lost on her.

In addition to the charm of its main character, the control of its lightly satirical tone, and its economy of execution, *A Fair Barbarian* demonstrates an ability which would later lift some of her children's books to the status of classics. She was able to draw out the fairy tale inherent in popular conventions and to edge her stories toward myth. This is most apparent in her portrayal of Lady Theobald, the social dragon whose tyranny over the old order is destroyed by Burnett's young female who represents the new order. With Lady Theobald, tyranny clearly begins at home, as she demonstrates by her upbringing of her orphaned niece, Lucia. This venerable lady adheres to "the good old school in which . . . it was customary to regard young people as weak, foolish, and if left to their own desires, frequently sinful" (210). Lucia's self-esteem has been almost eradicated by her aunt's regimen, and her suitor is probably not wide of the mark when he tells her, "If you had been a boy . . . and had squandered her money, and run into debt, and bullied her, you would have been her idol" (211). Lady Theobald's "old school" of education is overturned when Lucia copies Octavia's manner and dress; moreover, the lady's concept of hereditary social privilege is overthrown when Lucia marries a young mill-owner, a social parvenu who, like the frank American woman, has won the hearts of the rest of Slowbridge. The mythic role of this slain social dragon is punctuated by her final comment to her niece: "My rule is over. Permit me to congratulate you" (256).

A Fair Barbarian, like some of Burnett's later popular romances for adults and children, gives pause to a critic trying to assay the relative merit of her works and to conjecture about the degree to which she eventually realized her creative potential. On the one hand are works like *A Fair Barbarian* in which she fulfills or exceeds the limited expectations appropriate for light fiction, and on the other hand are works like *Haworth's* and even, though to a lesser extent, *That Lass o' Lowrie's,* in which she falls short of her more ambitious aims. Burnett's own perplexity about her career objectives at this juncture is reflected in her next novel, *Through One Administration,* the heroine of which is similarly divided between the "light" and "serious" sides of her personality. Though this realist novel contains a few vestiges from her "short 'easy' " love romances, it is for the most part a "big" book written to "please the critics," but, more important, to satisfy Burnett's own need to develop herself as a "serious" writer.

Through One Administration

Through One Administration, beginning serialization in November 1881 and published as a book in 1883, is a "big" book that causes a critic to wish Burnett had tried to extend herself further as a novelist later in her career. It is also the book which, perhaps more than any other, suggests the personal and professional reasons why she did—or could—not. Especially because of its portrayal of an unhappy Washington socialite—the most complex character in all of Burnett's fiction—*Through One Administration* deserves more attention than it has received in studies of American realism, especially that of the 1870s and 1880s which so often, as in the novels of William Dean Howells, Henry James, and Henry Adams, focused on women who were trying to stretch beyond their traditional roles. The novel's place within this tradition as well as its inherent value was recognized by its contemporary reviewers. The understatement of its unhappy ending was declared worthy, with minor qualifications, of Howells.[33] Reviewers also compared Burnett's portrayal of corruption in the nation's capital to that in *Democracy* by Henry Adams.[34] However, an *Athenaeum* reviewer correctly identified a closer resemblance to James's *Portrait of a Lady* (1881), serialized in the *Atlantic Monthly* as Burnett was working on *Through One Administration*.

As the *Athenaeum* reviewer recognized, Burnett's novelistic technique owed a great deal to James. Running well over five hundred pages, *Through One Administation* was her longest work so far; Burnett undoubtedly tried to imitate James when he "beautifully . . . goes all round a thing," as she had earlier put it. In citing the resemblance to James, the *Athenaeum* reviewer noted Burnett's "method of analysis, the attention to details, and the brilliancy and cleverness displayed in the conversations." He also observed that, like James, Burnett portrays characters who have a "tendency to an excessive refinement of sensitiveness."[35] In subject matter as well as technique Burnett is closer to James than to Adams. Though Adams's corrupt Senator Ratcliffe has a parallel in Burnett's Senator Planefield, her "female lobbyist" more closely resembles James's Isabel Archer, in *Portrait of a Lady,* than Adams's Madeleine Lee. Burnett uses corruption in Washington politics as primarily a "malarial" background— the image probably came from *Daisy Miller*—for her exploration of a woman's reaction when she learns she has chosen the wrong husband, a man whose effete values and selfish willingness to manipulate others make him a less-formidable Gilbert Osmond.

Bertha Amory is similar to Isabel Archer in that her romantic imagination and lack of experience cause her to overestimate her future husband and to marry him for the wrong reasons. Bertha regards the dilettante Richard Amory as "picturesque and pathetic—and poetic," and she marries him more out of "the fascination of making him happy" than deep affection for him (chap. 8). Soon after her marriage, she learns that she is only one of his dozens of enthusiasms and that he would not have been unhappy long if she had rejected him. However, she is "strong and weak enough" (chap. 8) to abide by her mistake, as her father says; she has the combination of character traits likely to make her a "martyr," if not a "saint": "cleverness," "conscience," "emotions," and "curiously obstinate and lofty views of the conduct of women who . . . [do] not hold their emotions neatly in check" (chaps. 1, 8). She suffers bouts of depression during the early years when her three children are born, but then she proudly and cleverly hides her unhappiness under the "light" and "frivolous" mask her shallow husband adores. She is careful of her children and punctilious in her conjugal role: She never speaks ungently to Amory, always dresses prettily for him, and treats him like a "Grand Pasha" (chap. 10). She keeps her mind off her unhappiness by wearing herself out with a constant "round" of social "gayeties [*sic*]"; and she almost convinces herself that, because her husband is totally satisfied with her and lets her have her way in everything, she is happy.

Bertha's program of self-control begins to break down, however, when a distant cousin, Colonel Philip Trendennis, returns to Washington after eight years of duty on the Western frontier. Philip threatens her controlled "lightness" at first because he reminds her of the self she was when he last saw her, an innocent young woman about to enter society and unable to imagine that she could ever be unhappy. Eventually, however, she realizes that they love each other, and she believes that if she had married this hulking, unfashionable, but noble soldier, she could have been "serious" and happy. Since her "lofty views of the conduct of women" have convinced her that her love for a man other than her husband makes her "wicked" (chap. 42), Bertha hides her love from Philip and tries to kill his love by making him believe that she really is the frivolous woman she appears. She hopes that if he rejects her, her pride will be injured and she will cease loving him.

Much of the fascination of Burnett's fictional heroine lies in the variety of faces she shows Philip as she covers herself with deceptions as multicolored as her fans. Because she respects as well as loves Philip, she cannot always hide from him the "serious" self she knows he loves. One face of this loved self is her devotion to her children, which she usually tries to hide by suggesting that, like the stereotypical lady of fashion, she is far more amused by the ballroom than the nursery. She allows herself one extended holiday from this mask when Philip visits her Virginia farmhouse retreat to help nurse her sick daughter—Bertha's husband is too far away on a business trip to come. After the child is well, Bertha and Philip enjoy an idyll of domesticity in nature, but they commit no transgressions against Ber-

tha's marriage. Though Bertha is by now fully aware of their mutual
love, Philip is blinded by his belief—sanctioned by Bertha's father—
that she is in love with Laurence Arbuthnot, another of her inner circle of admirers. Besides, Philip Trendennis's rigorous standards of
conduct would not permit him an indiscretion. Throughout the
novel, he adopts the stance of chivalric protector, ready to help but
making no special claims on her affection. Repeatedly referred to by
other characters as the survival of an earlier era of masculinity, Trendennis is most clearly a figure from medieval romance—though
Thackeray's Major Dobbin in *Vanity Fair* probably provided a more
immediate model.

The fascination of Bertha Amory's many faces lies not solely in her
strategy to kill Philip's love. Some of her faces suggest that her unhappiness occurs not totally because she finds herself acting out that
"old, miserable, undignified story of a woman who is married and
who cares for a man who is not her husband," as she puts it. Her
predicament is intensified because she is cast in the role of the
woman. "It is a curious thing, isn't it," she says, "that somehow one
always feels as if the woman must be bad" (chap. 22). It would not
be difficult to string together a series of quotations from *Through One
Administration* to make it seem a feminist critique of conventional
roles for women, for there are other passages implying that Bertha's
suffering is characteristically female. For example, Bertha once compares her controlled gaiety to that of "a man who was broken on the
wheel, and while it was being done he laughed, and shrieked, and
sang." "I think all women are like that sometimes," she adds (chap.
24). Bertha's father, often a touchstone in the novel, makes the similar observation that "women are not happy, as a rule" (chap. 8). This
unhappiness results partially from men's unrealistic expectations for
women. As Bertha tells Philip, "You have an ideal for everything
. . . especially for women, I think. You are always telling yourself
that they are good, and pure, and loving, and faithful; that they
adore their children, and are true to their friends. It is very pretty,
but it is not always the fact. You try to believe it is true of me; but
it is not. I am not your ideal woman" (chap. 24). Such statements
may be part of the mask Bertha uses to deceive Trendennis, but earlier in the scene the reader has heard her plan to adopt the strategy
of the diplomat who always mystified everyone by simply telling the
truth. It is not always easy to tell when Bertha is adopting this
strategy.

The question of appearance and reality in Bertha's character is further enhanced by comparisons of her situation to melodrama and by emphasizing the costumes she wears to play her various roles. Early in the novel, she flaunts her theatrical talents to her husband who has just told her he is entirely satisfied by the "clever and pretty" way she plays her role as a wife (chap. 10). She declares that she has neither of these qualities. "I haven't an attraction, really, but my gowns and my spirits and my speciousness," she tells Richard. "I am bold enough to adapt my gowns in such a way as to persuade you that I am physically responsible for the color and shape of them. You fancy you are pleased with me when you are simply pleased with some color of which I exist on the reflection or glow" (chap. 10). During the course of the novel, Bertha wears several colors suggesting her various personalities or roles. She dons white to suggest the hopeful innocence of her girlhood; the brilliant colors of a tropical bird to bedazzle most of her husband's friends; unadorned black to reveal her pallor and increasing slenderness to Laurence Arbuthnot, who understands her unhappiness; and dove-gray to suggest domestic "candor and simplicity" (chap. 31) when with her father, Philip, and a similarly chivalric admirer, Senator Blundel.

At times, indeed, it appears that Bertha herself is not sure when she is acting but that she is rather donning one costume after another to find out for herself who she really is. For the novel's reader, at any rate, there remains considerable ambiguity about when Bertha is feigning and when she is expressing what she considers her truest self, since Burnett rarely gives direct indications of Bertha's motives. Much of the story is narrated over the shoulder of Trendennis, who is also trying to figure Bertha out—much as James had portrayed Daisy Miller from Winterbourne's point of view. Most of Bertha's observations about herself are made to other characters, and the reader must judge the degree of candor she is likely to display to each—her husband, Trendennis, her father, Laurence Arbuthnot, and Agnes Sylvestre, who is her best female friend and feminine ideal. Like Isabel Archer, Bertha Amory is surrounded by characters whose chief "object" seems to be watching her. In addition to her father, who makes the serious mistake of misreading the object of Bertha's love, only two of these are fairly consistent in eliciting the truth from Bertha and in making accurate observations about her—Laurence Arbuthnot, who understands Bertha because he also uses a facade of "lightness" to hide his pain and pessimism; and the widow Agnes

Sylvestre, whose female intuition and previous unhappy marriage allow her to understand Bertha's suffering. None of these watchers,
however, is able to give Bertha much beyond sympathy; they are not
able to guide her out of what seems an entrapment in her various
disguises.

The question of Bertha's attitude toward her guises, as well as of
Burnett's critique of conventional and unconventional female roles,
depends largely on one's interpretation of Bertha's obedience to her
husband, her activities as a lobbyist, her ultrafeminine manner, and
her devotion to her children. In the matter of her obedience to her
husband, Bertha's play acting, as so often, seems to reveal as much
as it conceals. Early in the novel, she amuses her inner circle of
friends with a theatrical performance. "Enter the domestic virtues,"
she announces, as she appears before them with "work-basket on her
arm, . . . mob-cap upon her head, . . . apron around her waist, and
a plain square of white muslin crossed upon her bosom" (chap. 13).
Unfortunately, this gay little act of domestic servitude only foreshadows her later, serious practice of the art.

Her husband, Richard, has moved beyond his usual, safe role as
enthusiastic amateur at politics. Without Bertha's knowledge, he has
invested her fortune in iron-rich Westoria lands and is now lobbying
Congress to have a railroad built to make the lands accessible. Bertha
does not like the unsavory set of friends Richard now brings home,
but her belief that a wife should always support her husband's career
causes her to become his lobbyist, to beguile them in her home.
Though she does not know that it contains a bribe, she agrees to give
a letter to the influential Senator Blundel, who has become infatuated
by her dove-gray appearances before him. Blundel is convinced that
she is unaware of the letter's contents as well as of Richard's financial
investment in the scheme. And so, in a chivalric gesture, he burns
the letter; and he also escorts her to a charity ball to advertise her
innocence in the scandal. With the help of her friends, Bertha braves
the hostile stares, but this social triumph coincides with her personal
defeat. When she returns home from the ball, she learns that Richard
has fled abroad, leaving her to face alone the financial loss as well as
the scandal. There is an irony almost tragic in Bertha's defeat. It is
precisely her exaggerated willingness to help her husband that brings
about their eventual separation; for, without Bertha's help, Richard
knew that his lobbying could not succeed and probably would not

have ventured so much. Viewed retrospectively, Bertha's earlier tableau of domestic servitude has a humor more grim than gay.

Of course, Bertha's defeat could be attributed not so much to her conjugal obedience as to her venturing outside the conventional female realm to become a lobbyist. The traditional view that men and women have separate domains is presented by Senator Blundel. From a woman, he expects "rest and light recreation, . . . relief from . . . the ambitious world he lived in." The women he knew as a boy "spent the most of their time with their children," and he declares that "they were pretty good women" and "did very little mischief." Blundel does admit, however, that these women "got old pretty soon, and lost their good looks"; and, he adds, "I shouldn't like to be a woman myself, and have to follow my leader, and live in one groove from beginning to end" (chap. 34).

Bertha's own attitude toward her political activities is equally ambiguous. For the most part, she plays along with those who see her interest in politics as an attractive "pet pretense" (chap. 9). But one wonders if, like the successful diplomat, she is not telling the truth when she says to Trendennis, "I should like to feel that anything so important [as the Westoria lands] depended on me. . . . I should like the sense of power." When Trendennis reminds her that she is attributed power "far more than most women," she says that such power is "too trivial. It is only a matter of pleasing or displeasing. . . . It does not enable me to bestow things" (chap. 20). She has apparently discarded as unsuited to her temperament that exercise of "power" to "bestow things" outside of the home which the nineteenth-century found more appropriate for women, charitable activities. In another scene, she tells Philip, "If I were religious, I should have Dorcas societies and missions" instead of lobbying (chap. 24).

Whatever Bertha's attitude toward contemporary avenues for female power may be, by the end of the novel she has reason to agree with Blundel's sad conclusion that "this isn't an easy world" (chap. 34). For if Bertha finds herself unprepared for her foray into the male domain of politics, she also learns that taking refuge in traditional female roles does not guarantee safety. For example, her obedience to her husband is accompanied by an ostrichlike retreat into an ultra-feminine ideal. She jests merrily about her ignorance about business matters as she signs without reading it the document which allows her husband to invest her money in the Westoria lands. Burnett offers another critique of this ultrafeminine ideal through the "purely feminine apartment" Bertha fits out in her home for Agnes Sylvestre. Described mainly by the satiric Laurence Arbuthnot, the apartment is both pink and blue so as to compliment both blondes and brunettes; its mirror is positioned to reflect light to the viewer's advantage; and it has lots of lace and "openly sentimental" pictures (chap. 22). In some ways, this room does provide a female refuge. Men may not enter it, and it is the scene for an all-night vigil between Bertha and Agnes. The chapter set here, in which the women analyze their unhappiness as women, provides the novel's most extended portrayal of Bertha's point of view. On the other hand, Arbuthnot's description of the room points to the dangerous narcissism as well as "lightness of mind" (chap. 22) implicit in the ultrafeminine ideal. As Bertha's unwillingness to concern herself with business demonstrates, a woman seeks refuge in this ideal at her own peril.

Burnett makes more efforts to be sympathetic toward another traditional female refuge, the nursery. In urging Bertha to curtail her social and political activities, her friends have little success with appeals to her own declining health. In part, this is because her guilt about her love for Philip takes a masochistic or, as she puts it, "morbid," turn. "I was a wicked woman," she tells her father in confessing this love; "do you think that I shall some day have been punished enough?" (chap. 42). Appeals based on her responsibility to her children have more success in persuading Bertha to slow down, and she claims that it is only her desire to protect them from scandal that prompts her to go to the ball and exonerate herself. Moreover, it is in the nursery with her children that she takes her final refuge— "the only safe thing . . . for a woman who is unhappy," as she earlier observed (chap. 34).

As the novel ends, Bertha and her children are living with her father; she has refused the money Philip had offered to offset her financial loss, though she does allow him to put it into a trust for her daughter Janey. Convinced that he can no longer help Bertha, Philip has returned to the Western frontier; Richard is still in Paris, hopeful about his next speculative venture and vague about the date of his return to his family. In the last chapter, Bertha goes to an inaugural ball during which word arrives that Philip has been killed during an Indian raid. Bertha's father takes her home and watches her climb the dark stairs to the nursery. The novel concludes with the statement that "Bertha went into the room and closed the door." Despite Burnett's earlier attempts to suggest that Bertha is her most genuine, happy, and virtuous self when she is with her children, the tone of this ending makes the nursery seem far more the refuge of last resort than the place where a woman embraces her most self-fulfilling role. Moreover, there are suggestions that this refuge is regressive; since Bertha is returning to her father's home and protection, she is returning not only to her children's nursery but her own.

An *Atlantic* reviewer in 1883 exaggerated only a little when he said that *Through One Administration,* "when all is said, is a brilliant book. It might have been a great one."[36] If the book is closer to being "brilliant" than her previous novels, it is primarily because in it Burnett allowed herself to portray some of her own deepest conflicts as a woman and as a writer. In her portrayal of Bertha, Burnett consciously or unconsciously revealed much about her own unhappiness in marriage. Even before she was married, she had given Swan concern about her restlessness when she postponed their wedding to take a fifteen-month trip to England. After they were married, she compensated by signing a contract with *Peterson's* which enabled them to live in Paris, where Swan wanted to study. Especially after they returned, however, Swan was ambivalent about her career. He exhibited pride in her accomplishments and handled all her business affairs; however, according to Thwaite, he also had difficulty accepting her breadwinning role and was often impatient that her career took her so often away from home.

One of these career trips, Thwaite conjectures, also represented a more intimate threat to their marriage. During the summer of 1881, she packed her incomplete manuscript of *Through One Administration* and went to New York. She spent some time at a seaside resort with William Gillette, who was helping her finish her dramatization of *Esmeralda.* During this stay, Burnett apparently had a sensual "awakening" similar to that of the married heroine of Kate Chopin's later novel, for in a letter to a female friend, Burnett described the body of a swimming instructor and declared, "I never noticed a man's body before."[37] The most serious threat to Burnett's marriage, however, Thwaite conjectures, was Burnett's increasing intimacy with her editor at Scribner's, Richard Watson Gilder, who was also married. During this same summer, the two had "lovely times" during an overnight trip to the beach, which Burnett described in another letter to her friend. Since this episode apparently marked the end of the close relationship between Burnett and Gilder, Thwaite infers that their mutual affection had become serious enough to threaten their marriages.[38]

In addition to this possible biographical basis for Bertha's love for a man other than her husband, Burnett, like Bertha, suffered bouts of depression and vague physical illnesses, apparently beginning early in her marriage. In 1876, at least—just four weeks before Vivian was born and shortly after she had finished *That Lass o' Lowrie's*—Burnett expressed her depression in an unpublished poem. In it, a wife conjectures that if she would die, her husband would not understand why "the end came and why I wearied so."[39] Thwaite also notes that it was during these early years that Burnett wrote her stories of female suicides. Understandably, in his biography of his mother, Vivian Burnett handles more gingerly the autobiographical bases for *Through One Administration*. He notes that some of the characters were modeled on Burnett's friends in Washington, but says that "she was not consciously putting herself into the book." "Bertha's situation, in the book, was entirely fictitious," Vivian declares, but he does allow that "the manner in which she expressed herself about it was very much the Frances Hodgson Burnett of 1880." Always protective of his father, Vivian says that Burnett took "certain physical characteristics" of her husband "and imagined a wretched soul to go with them, which she paraded through the book as Richard Amory."[40]

Through One Administration reveals not only Burnett's conflicts about her marriage but also the dilemma she faced in deciding the course of her future career. By now she knew that with little effort she could toss off "short 'easy' " books like *A Fair Barbarian* and be fairly sure that they would reward her financially. Writing "serious" books to satisfy the critics of "actual literature," however, would be more draining not only in the time and energy required for writing them but also in continuing the reading program necessary to compensate for the deficiencies in her dame school education. Burnett's marital problems could only exacerbate this dilemma, for if she put less of herself into her writing, she might better be able to live up to the ideal Swan—and she herself—had for a wife and mother. Burnett's career dilemma is reflected in Bertha's indecision about whether to be the "light" person her husband wants or the "serious" person she wants to be. Being "light" and "frivolous"—writing clever romances—is the method Bertha adopts to play her role as a faithful wife. Being "serious"—writing the energy-consuming and possibly self-revelatory "big" books—represents a threat to Bertha's marriage since it not only displeases her husband but also encourages her lover. Like Bertha the socialite, Burnett the writer was no doubt haunted by the suspicion that she was "too clever." And she was probably beginning to realize that "one gets so tired of it." Like Bertha, Burnett probably wished she "could stop thinking and know less—or more" (chap. 22). In *Through One Administration,* however, she decided to try to know "more." She would downplay her "clever" talent for writing fairy tales with happy endings and dramatize her own increasing sense that "it is very hard to live. . . . One can only go on—and on—and there is always something worse coming" (chap. 24).

If Burnett's ability to address her own deepest conflicts as a woman and a writer allowed *Through One Administration* to be called a "brilliant" book, her inability to resolve these conflicts can be accounted the main reason why the book did not become "a great one." *Through One Administration* is a book divided against itself. It is divided first of all because Burnett could not make up her mind about Bertha, as has already been suggested; she could not simply flirt with "the woman question" in her portrayal of this unhappy Washington socialite even as she could not explore the issue to its fullest. The book is divided also because she could not decide whether she was writing the kind of conventional romance she had already perfected in *A Fair Barbarian* or the realist novel that was struggling to be born in *That Lass o' Lowrie's* and *Haworth's.* She tried to have it both ways and it did not work. It might be argued, of course, that these divisions were caused not by her own inability to resolve her conflicts but by her desire to reach as wide an audience as possible. She could hedge on "the woman question" and perhaps satisfy readers on both sides. There would be something in the book for the readers of her light romances and for the critics of "actual literature," too. As shown especially by her later career, Burnett did have a genius for knowing what readers wanted and she often enough demonstrated a willingness to provide it. Such calculation may have played a minor role in causing the division within *Through One Administration,* but the much greater role of her own indecision is argued not only by the nature of her personal conflicts at the time she wrote it but also by the fact that during the three years after she finished it, she continued to be unwell; and her pen, which had moved steadily for thirteen years, stopped completely.

While the biographer may wish to speculate further about the reasons for the divisions within *Through One Administration,* the primary task of the critic is to point out and to estimate their effect on the book's quality. Repeated careful readings of the novel suggest that Burnett wished to attribute Bertha's unhappiness primarily to her having married the wrong man. This interpretation would have us believe that if Bertha had married Philip instead of Richard, she would have been happy within the conventional limits set for the life of a wife and mother; her enthusiasm for social gaieties and politics were only methods for diverting her gaze from her unhappy marriage or they were pretenses to please her husband and drive her lover away. The problem with this reading, of course, is that Bertha's methods and pretenses are all too convincing. Burnett's execution contradicts her apparent intentions also in her portrayal of Agnes Sylvestre. On the one hand, Burnett gives this female paragon the rewards she denies to the venturesome Bertha. Death has saved Agnes from her morally deficient husband, and her quiet resignation to unhappiness is rewarded with a compatible new mate in Laurence Arbuthnot. Without irony, Burnett portrays Agnes as "fair, feminine, full of all tender sympathy and kindly thought; not ignorant of the world nor bitter against it, only bearing no stain of it upon her" (chap. 25), and Burnett elsewhere comments that Agnes needs only her "passion-colored" eyes to communicate her full womanhood (chap. 31). Agnes strikes the reader as a hortatory illustration from *Peterson's* compared to the multi-dimensional Bertha, who cannot decide whether to be the frivolous child-bride Dora in *David Copperfield* or the worldly adventuress Becky Sharp in *Vanity Fair* (chaps. 2, 13).

Burnett's comparative portrayal of Agnes and Bertha illustrates not only the book's division on "the woman question" but also its often incongruous mixture of light love romance and serious, realist novel. In the story of Agnes, Burnett uses the typed characters, comic sense of life, and happy ending of romance, while in the story of Bertha, she uses the multifaceted characters, tragic sense of life, and understated unhappy ending of the realist novel. The two kinds of stories in the novel are vastly disproportionate in quality. The romance lacks the energy and cleverness of *A Fair Barbarian*, while some of the characterization and construction of the dominant plot built around Bertha make *Through One Administration* a significant realist advance over *That Lass o' Lowrie's* and *Haworth's*.

The best characterization in *Through One Administration* is elicited not by the interaction between lovers but that between friends, between antagonists, or between antagonistic selves within one person, as within Bertha and, to a lesser extent, Laurence Arbuthnot. Once again, Burnett's execution validates her statement that she detested love stories, for those in *Through One Administration* are artificial and overwritten. This is especially true of the courtship between Agnes and Laurence, a lifeless pastiche of conventions from Burnett's fiction in *Peterson's*. But we also hear far too much praise of Colonel Trendennis's "reverence for age, tenderness to womanhood and childhood, faithfulness to all things" (chap. 20), and we must wade through too many of his agonizing cogitations about Bertha, especially in the second half of the novel. In contrast, Burnett handles with deft strokes the repartee and the sympathetic understanding between Bertha and Laurence, whose friendship is based on similar personalities and views of life. Bertha and her husband are not portrayed together so often, but their combination of limited affection and inherent incompatibility is also convincing. Burnett avoids the pitfall of oversimplifying Richard Amory as a villain. He is charming enough to make the reader believe that an immature Bertha would marry him, and Burnett handles with some subtlety the stages by which he moves from naive enthusiasm to desperate self-protection in the Westoria affair. Perhaps because she was in part using her husband as a model, Burnett is more gentle with Amory than James was with Osmond.

The claims of *Through One Administration* on the realist tradition lie not only in some of its characterization but also in its effective portrayal of a world in which individuals' fates are determined largely by forces outside their control. There are repeated references to persons who lost their jobs to someone in greater favor with a powerful office holder, and to persons who lost their fortunes because their lobbying, legal as well as illegal, eventually failed—Bertha and Richard are not the first to lose money on the Westoria lands. The problems of staying afloat in a sea of corruptible power are compounded by the fact that in a democratic society power is constantly changing hands. Burnett calls attention to this fact through her title, *Through One Administration,* and by having most of her narration take place between the inauguration of one president and that of the next. To this narrative she adds a prologue which describes Bertha briefly over Philip Trendennis's shoulder. He visits her when she is a hopeful young woman about to go to her first ball and just before he is about to return to the frontier for a stay of eight years. Bertha's courtship, marriage, and discovery of her unhappiness in her marriage are thus described effectively from a distance, through occasional comments in her fa-

ther's letters to Philip and through her father's conversation with
Philip shortly after he returns to Washington during inaugural festiv-
ities early in the book.

Burnett's prologue to her "one administration" intends to show
that Bertha's fate, like the political fate of many in Washington, depends largely on whether the time is in or "out of joint."[41] As Bertha's father says, "the experience of a woman of forty is what a girl
needs when she chooses her husband at twenty, and, as the two
things are incompatible, the chances are always against her" (chap.
8). When she first meets Philip, Bertha is too young to measure the
integrity of this considerably older soldier against the social gaieties
which beckon just outside her door. When Philip returns to Washington with a new administration, it is too late to save Bertha from
the knowledge that "the worse [sic] punishments in life . . . are for
ignorance" (chap. 8). He is powerless to arrest her increasing perception that "nothing is of consequence" and that "no one is happy in
the world" (chap. 11).

In this most complex and ambitious of Burnett's novels, she was
faithful enough to her sense of Bertha as a realist character to know
that even a knight of medieval romance could not save her. Though
she does not make the comparison explicit, Philip Trendennis is a Sir
Lancelot with more fastidious morals.[42] Burnett's Lancelot goes to almost incredible lengths to save his Guinevere from the fires of her
love for him as well as the political fires her husband has built around
her: He denies his own desires not only in refusing to make special
claims on her affection but also in getting out of her way when his
presence disturbs her composure; he braves the ballroom battles he
dislikes to win friends who will help her when he cannot; and without her knowing it, he makes her husband an offer to offset the loss
of her fortune in the Westoria affair. Unlike the original Lancelot,
Philip is granted an heroic death in battle: He dies from an Indian's
arrow while he is rescuing a child from her burning house. This fiery
heroism has not been able to rescue Bertha, however. Wisely, Burnett does not give us Philip's thoughts as he died, but she does hint
at them through a story he had earlier told Bertha's daughter, Janey.
Combined with a reminder of Bertha's actions in the last lines of the
novel, Philip's story points to the realist critique of romance Burnett
allowed herself in the dominant part of *Through One Administration*.
As the knight in the story lay dying on the battlefield at night, he
looked at the sky and "wondered why he had been given his sword

and armor, and why he had been allowed to feel so strong, and glad, and eager—only for that" (chap. 34). Only for Bertha to climb the dark steps to the nursery, enter, and then "close . . . the door."

For three years after she finished *Through One Administration,* as has already been mentioned, Burnett like Bertha "closed the door" on her audience. She had reason to feel that she deserved a rest after thirteen years during which she had written numerous short stories, six novels, and two adaptations for the stage even as she had expanded her life to include a husband and two children and had had visits or residences in Tennessee, Long Island, New England, England, France, Washington, D.C. Moreover, this largely self-educated woman of thirty-two had reason to congratulate herself on her reception with the critics, who compared her work favorably to major writers on both sides of the Atlantic—Gaskell, Eliot, and C. Brontë; Howells, Adams, and James.

For a twentieth-century critic reassessing Burnett's achievement, it would provide at least some consolation to be able to believe that she enjoyed her rest after she had completed the novel which represents her most heroic attempt to confront herself in her writing and to stretch beyond the conventions of ladies' magazine fiction, her earliest tutors in learning her craft. For if *Through One Administration* lacks the steadiness of aim and execution, the intellectual and historical sophistication of Burnett's new mentors, Howells and especially James, it clearly deserves more than the near oblivion into which it has been cast by twentieth-century literary histories.[43] Unfortunately, however, when one considers the personal and professional dilemmas Burnett portrayed but did not fully resolve in *Through One Administration,* one has little reason to believe that Burnett was much happier than Bertha when she entered the nursery and "closed the door." One senses rather that Burnett sought the nursery as a refuge from her unhappy marriage and that while there she continued to wrestle with her "light" and "serious" literary faces. When she stepped outside again in 1885, she brought *Little Lord Fauntleroy* with her; and the phenomenal reception of this nursery hero would help her decide whether to develop her talents for writing realist novels or romances.

Chapter Three
Popular Romances for Children and Adults (1885–99)

The phenomenal popularity and financial success of *Little Lord Fauntleroy* (1886) and its stage adaptation (1888) proved a turning point in Burnett's career. Though some of her subsequent fiction would provide detailed portrayals of life in a specific locality and address contemporary issues, as did *That Lass o' Lowrie's* and *Through One Administration,* Burnett abandoned her earlier attempts as a serious realist novelist to devote herself to popular romances for children and adults.

From 1885 to 1899, Burnett wrote three kinds of popular romances she would also write later. The first, exemplified by *Little Lord Fauntleroy,* could be called the child romance since in it Burnett used the Cinderella plot formula from her earlier love romances and took personality traits from her good coquettes to create its innocent child hero. During the decade following *Little Lord Fauntleroy,* most of Burnett's publications were either for or about children. Nothing of what she wrote for children matched that romance in quality or popularity, but she effectively captured childhood perceptions and experience in her memoir, *The One I Knew the Best of All* (1893). Taken collectively, Burnett's writing during this decade provided a background of literary portrayals of the child that would culminate in her later children's classics, *A Little Princess* and *The Secret Garden.*

The second kind of popular romance Burnett wrote from 1885 to 1899 was the love romance, which had provided her earliest entry into publishing. During her decade of writing almost exclusively for or about the child, Burnett published three short love romances, *A Woman's Will,* or *Miss Defarge* (1887), *The Fortunes of Philippa Fairfax* (1888), and *The Pretty Sister of José* (1889). Her wholehearted return to adult fiction, however, was signaled by her first best-seller after

Little Lord Fauntleroy, A Lady of Quality (1896), immediately followed by a companion volume, *His Grace of Osmonde* (1897).

The third kind of popular romance Burnett wrote during this period can be called the "social melodrama," the term John G. Cawelti uses to describe popular novels combining formulas from popular fiction with the realist's detailed, often panoramic portrayal of a recent or contemporary world.[1] Set in America immediately before and after the Civil War, *In Connection with The De Willoughby Claim* (1899) previewed similar best-selling romances for adults Burnett would write later, such as *The Shuttle*.

Early Stories for Children and *Little Lord Fauntleroy*

Although in writing for children Burnett adapted plot formulas and character types she had used in writing love romances, other influences can be identified through a brief examination of four stories she published in the children's magazine, *St. Nicholas,* before and immediately after *Little Lord Fauntleroy* was serialized in that magazine in 1885, the year before it appeared as a book. Throughout her life Burnett loved to tell or read stories to children. She told her own children "Hair Curling Stories," which got their label not from their thrilling content but from their being told to keep her boys quiet while she curled their hair.[2] The unintentionally absurd fantasy, "The Proud Little Grain of Wheat" (January 1880), was probably one such story since it mentions Lionel and Vivian by name.

As might be expected, Burnett was also influenced by the fairy tale, as demonstrated by "The Story of Prince Fairyfoot" (December 1886–February 1887), a retelling of a tale from an anthology Burnett had loved as a child, Frances Browne's *Granny's Wonderful Chair* (1856). Born with tiny feet in a kingdom of folk proud of their huge feet, Prince Fairyfoot escapes to a country whose citizens also have small feet like his; aided by two fairies, self-important Robin Goodfellow and his saucy lover, Gauzeta, Prince Fairyfoot marries the princess of the new country and lives happily ever after. Prince Fairyfoot's character type greatly appealed to Burnett—someone different from and usually superior to his or her surroundings. Such had been many of her earlier Cinderella-like coquettes and working-class Junos as well as later, of course, Little Lord Fauntleroy himself, whose innate nobility is evident even when he sits on a keg in a New York

City grocery store. Although clever in spots, "The Story of Prince Fairyfoot," like her other early fantasies, confirms what would become evident in her later career as well: She was far more successful when she used fairy tales to enrich stories set in an idealized real world than when she imitated them more directly in fantasy.

The best-known of these early stories, "Editha's Burglar" (February 1880), adapted for the stage as *Nixie* (1890), indicates that Burnett was also influenced by a more somber kind of story often given to children, the religious or moral exemplum. In her memoir, Burnett criticizes tales in which child saints die with pious sayings on their lips, but she says that as a child she had been much affected by them—law-abiding and earnest, she would have given anything to have been considered an example. The seven-year-old heroine of "Editha's Burglar" succeeds where its author as a child had failed. Editha asks a burglar to be quiet so as not to awaken her mother, and she brings her own pretty things so that he will not take her parents' possessions. At the end of the story, Editha's mother pledges to pay more attention to her child, and the burglar returns her treasures. As an exemplary child, Editha is a prototype for Little Lord Fauntleroy and some of Burnett's later fictional children; earnest, emotionally precocious, and imaginative, they often associate primarily with adults for whom they feel protective and on whom they have a beneficent effect.

All of these influences—her own children, the tales she told them, her memory of herself as a child, the fairy tale, and the exemplum— plus her early Cinderella love romances, played a role in the creation of *Little Lord Fauntleroy*. In addition, Burnett's early stories show an awareness of significant changes in children's literature at the time. She was apparently prompted to publish for children by meeting Louisa May Alcott, the author of *Little Women* (1865), and Mary Mapes Dodge, the editor of *St. Nicholas,* at a Papyrus Club dinner in Boston, in 1879. The stories she wrote for Dodge's magazine suggest that she had also read the works of Lewis Carroll and George Mac-Donald. "Behind the White Brick" (January 1879) shows the influence of Carroll's *Alice* books; in Burnett's story, a little girl falls asleep, visits a fantasy realm behind a brick in a chimney, and is guided by a saucy baby reminiscent of the imperious creatures in Carroll's Wonderland. The lightly satirical tone and suggestion of a moral in "The Story of Prince Fairyfoot" invite comparison to MacDonald's literary fairy tale, "The Light Princess" (1864, 1867)—

Burnett had met MacDonald on her honeymoon trip to New York. And while Burnett's idealized children owed much to her childhood reading of exempla, she may have been encouraged to use this character type by MacDonald's spiritually precocious child in *At the Back of the North Wind* (1871).

Burnett undoubtedly welcomed the new spirit in children's literature evidenced by Carroll and MacDonald, with their use of the fairy tale and fantasy and their romantic idealization of the child; for in her memoir, Burnett says that as a child she had not much liked the earlier, more didactic writers such as Anna Barbauld, Maria Edgeworth, and Peter Parley; she had preferred adventure romances not written specifically for children, by authors such as Sir Walter Scott, Harrison Ainsworth, and James Fenimore Cooper (*O,* chaps. 4, 7). Best-sellers in America during the 1880s—*Treasure Island* (1883), *Huckleberry Finn* (1885), and *King Solomon's Mines* (1886)—demonstrate an increasing popular interest in the romance and the child; with her instinct for knowing what the public wanted, Burnett probably knew that the time was right for a book which combined the two. Apparently unable to write another "big" book like *Through One Administration,* Burnett undoubtedly recognized, consciously or unconsciously, that she could adapt the Cinderella formula from her adult love romances to write a "short 'easy' "[3] book for children that would probably find an adult audience as well.

Burnett gives her own account of how she came to write her famous best-seller in "How Fauntleroy Occurred and a Very Real Little Boy Became an Ideal One" (1894). The essay describes her young son Vivian, and the parallels between Vivian and the fictional Cedric Errol are many. Taken as a whole, however, the essay demonstrates how fiction and fact became inextricably mixed in her creative process, how fictional formulas became a lens through which she apprehended the world. As she herself elsewhere put it, "All my life I have made stories, and since I was seven years old I have written them. This has been my way of looking at life as it went by me."[4] Perhaps most telling is her description of how her observations of Vivian so quickly and easily turned into story formula. Always impressed by her son's "republican" generosity, which took no account of social class, Burnett one day wondered how he would strike a haughty English nobleman. "Eureka!" she cried. "Son of a younger son, separated from ill-tempered noble father because he has married a poor young American beauty. Young father dead, elder brothers dead, boy comes

into title! Yes, there it is, and Vivian shall be he. . . . A story like
that is easily written."[5]

"How Fauntleroy Occurred" also demonstrates how fictional formula often became a lens through which Burnett perceived herself.
Though she often smiles at herself as a doting mother, she portrays
herself in the essay very much like the idealized mother, "Dearest,"
in *Little Lord Fauntleroy*. At the end of *Through One Administration,*
Bertha Amory had closed the door on her quandary about whether
she wanted to be Dora Copperfield or Becky Sharp. "How Fauntleroy
Occurred" and *Little Lord Fauntleroy* suggest that Burnett took refuge
from her own marital and career dilemmas by adopting another fictional ideal, Thackeray's Amelia Sedley. Indeed, the situation of
"Dearest" in *Little Lord Fauntleroy* seems directly derived from *Vanity
Fair*. Like Amelia Sedley, "Dearest" is a poor widow who must give
her beloved son to the charge of his irascible paternal grandfather,
who can give him more worldly advantages.

Little Lord Fauntleroy demonstrates the talent for light romance that
Burnett had earlier shown in *A Fair Barbarian,* similarly dramatizing
a young American who overcomes the prejudices of a haughty British
aristocracy. Like the adult romance, *Little Lord Fauntleroy* relies on
typed characters—the idealized child and mother; the misanthropic,
aristocratic grandfather; the Dickensian commoners. For a child audience, however, Burnett gives her characters bolder outline; and the
presumed necessity for more action in the plot of children's stories
allows more rein for her earlier-touted "art as a storyteller." This art
as well as Burnett's ability to tap the narrative and thematic power of
the fairy tale allows *Little Lord Fauntleroy,* as well as her later children's classics, *A Little Princess* and *The Secret Garden,* to survive their
occasional sentimentality.

Characterization and plot development in *Little Lord Fauntleroy* resemble that in the fairy tale. Faithful to the archetypal Cinderella
story which underlies her romance, Burnett does not portray an internal change in her main character. As is the case with Cinderella,
changes occur only in Cedric Errol's external circumstances as the
world gradually recognizes his innate nobility. Like many a fairy tale,
Burnett's romance dramatizes the tests by which the hero demonstrates his worth; Cedric must prove himself incorruptible by wealth
and title before he receives them. His grandfather's largesse must not
mar his love for his mother or his sympathy for the less fortunate;
and when his worldly possessions are threatened by the appearance of

an imposter heir, he must accept their potenial loss with equanimity. When he also manages to tame the monster in his den—he transforms a selfish old man into an affectionate grandfather and responsible landlord—Little Lord Fauntleroy's heroic innocence is established without qualification.

Little Lord Fauntleroy's subsequently maligned beauty is thus of a piece with his portrayal as the hero of a fairy tale or heroic romance. Like Cinderella's, his beauty is an outward sign of his inner nature. A large part of the book's notoriety resulted because too many parents, who had read the book or had seen Burnett's play, did not respect the crucial lines between fiction and fact implied by the story's genre; much of the animosity against Fauntleroy as a sissy must have come from the children who were forced to wear velvet and lace. Burnett herself was partly to blame, of course. She let it be known that Reginald Birch's illustrations for the book were based on a photograph of Vivian; she was not above cashing in on the Fauntleroy phenomenon by endorsing related products such as playing cards and candy; and she loved to play the role of "Dearest" in her backstage life with the children who starred in her play.[6] If she often herself failed to make a sharp distinction between fiction and fact, however, she was quick to point to it in the defense of her own children. To scotch rumors that her boys paraded as fops, she reported to the press that they were "strong, manly, robust" creatures who as often as not wore clothes made ragged by rough play.[7] Such protestations however, did not keep Burnett's fictional boy from coming to epitomize the sentimentality about children which marked much popular literature and culture at the time.

In some ways this reputation is not completely fair. For if Burnett enjoyed being "Dearest" to little Elsie Leslie, who played Little Lord Fauntleroy in America, Mark Twain embroidered a slipper for the same actress; and in London, Lewis Carroll grieved that his own current favorite did not get the role.[8] James Barrie's 1904 play, *Peter Pan*, purveyed a more sentimental view of childhood than did Burnett's romance. While Burnett portrayed adults sympathetically, alluded to Little Lord Fauntleroy's adult role as an earl and insisted in "How Fauntleroy Occurred" that her son Vivian was happily growing up into a young man, Barrie's play satirized adults and portrayed a boy who disdains growing up.

Twentieth-century film adaptations of *Little Lord Fauntleroy* show that a taste for idealized fictional children has not disappeared, especially when combined with the popular appeal of the fairy tale. In 1914 a British company made a film following close to the original story. In 1921 America's Sweetheart, Mary Pickford, played both Cedric and his mother in a silent film using trick photography. In 1936, David O. Selznick found in Burnett's story justification for displaying a panoply of Hollywood stars, including Freddie Bartholomew and Mickey Rooney. And finally, in 1980, Norman Rosemont attracted Sir Alec Guiness as well as Ricky Schroder to star in a movie for television. Burnett's *Little Lord Fauntleroy* must be accounted a significant contribution not only to children's literature but also to popular culture.

Other Writing for Children

Most of Burnett's writing for children in the decade following *Little Lord Fauntleroy* took the form of sketches, short fiction, and essays for various magazines; many of these pieces appeared in three collections: *Little Saint Elizabeth and Other Stories* (1890), *Giovanni and the Other* (1892), and *Piccino and Other Stories* (1894). The only longer works she published were her memoir in 1893, and a narrative description of the Chicago World's Fair, *Two Little Pilgrims' Progress* (1895).

Burnett's stories and sketches share with *Little Lord Fauntleroy* a romantic view of children. The main character of "Sara Crewe" (*St. Nicholas,* December 1887–February 1888) is not so idealized as she would be in the later, expanded version, *A Little Princess;*[9] but the title character in "Little Saint Elizabeth" (*St. Nicholas,* December 1888–January 1889) is a sister to the earlier Editha and Cedric Errol. Steeped in saints legends when she lived with her ascetic aunt in Normandy, the saintly Elizabeth has difficulty adjusting to the worldly life of her bachelor uncle in New York. Her relationship with him resembles that between the conscientious Elsie Dinsmore and her less pious father in Margaret Finlay's famous contemporary series; Burnett's saintly Elizabeth takes upon herself the charitable activities her secular uncle neglects. One cold day she faints on the street after giving her coat to a poor woman, and her subsequent illness makes her uncle more sympathetic to the poor while it helps her accept the benefits of his wealth. The story criticizes the ascetic ideal for children upheld in moral and religious exempla. Though Elizabeth "lost none of her sweet sympathy for those who suffered," Burnett's narrator concludes that the little girl "learned to live a more natural and childlike life, and to find that there were in the world innocent, natural pleasures which should be enjoyed."[10]

Burnett's romantic concept of the "natural and childlike life" is as much pagan as Christian, as shown by some of the stories and sketches in *Giovanni and the Other* and *Piccino and Other Child Stories*. In "The Pretty Roman Beggar" and "The Little Faun," for example, Burnett describes rosy-cheeked children of the poor who, half-clad and dirty, play happily in the streets, oblivious of their social station. She attributes their joy to their "half-human, half-animal" nature like that of the classical fauns and dryads (*G,* 119). As the titles of these anthologies suggest, many of the stories are set in Italy, where Burnett recuperated after her oldest son died. She may have been encouraged to write about Italy also by her friendship there with the American writer Constance Fenimore Woolson, whose career in some ways paralleled Burnett's. Like Burnett, Woolson had written American local color stories and novels; then, after moving to Italy, she wrote stories about Americans there. Both writers knew Henry James, though Woolson's relationship with him was more intimate. Some of Burnett's Italian stories also grew out of her grief over Lionel's death. "Giovanni and the Other," for example, contains a self-indulgent self-portrait in its depiction of a wealthy tourist who, in memory of her dead son, supports a peasant boy who becomes a great singer. It is a sentimental and rather morbid tale—unfortunately, Burnett did not imitate Woolson's frequent understatement and restraint.

Burnett's view of Italy in her stories is, more than Woolson's, that of the tourist. In one story, however, she is mildly critical of one kind of tourist. In "Two Days in the Life of Piccino," a bored, wealthy English woman visiting the Riviera "borrows" a beautiful peasant boy who is understandably perturbed when she bathes and dresses him to parade before her guests. When the boy escapes and flees back home, the lady does not regret the loss: "She had found it too tiresome an amusement to undertake the management of the lovely little wild animal, to whom civilization only represented horror and dismay," and she regards him as only an "amusing" anecdote to relate to friends back in London (*P,* 76). The story does criticize one kind of tourist reaction to the Italian peasants—that they are dirty and uncivilized; but, like other stories in these anthologies, it purveys the opposite, sentimental view that they are picturesque. The author who had earlier portrayed at near eye level the lives of the miners in *That Lass o' Lowrie's* was now adopting the point of view of the wealthy and the aristocratic; and she balances her portrayals of beautiful children of the poor with portraits of wealthy and royal children, "Illustrissimo Signor Bébé" and "Eight Little Princes."[11] Burnett's conservative views about effecting social change are indicated by the mother's advice to a boy who, after reading Edward Bellamy's *Looking Backward,* tells her he has become a socialist. She tells him that "the great changes for the better are always made because a number of people make up their minds singly," and she reminds him that "a good Socialist" would pick up the clutter in his room and not leave the work for others (*G,* 143–46).

In addition to her short fiction and sketches, Burnett wrote some essays, probably commissioned. To a collection of essays addressed to the parents of boys, *Before He Is Twenty* (1894), she contributed a discussion of how a boy chooses a career. In this essay, as well as in "The Drury Lane Boys' Club," a description of her establishment of a library for poor children in London, Burnett compares the child to a plant or flower that needs careful cultivation. Similarly, there are pastoral themes in her description of Washington, D.C., "A City of Groves and Bowers" for the young readers of *St. Nicholas* (June 1893).

Two Little Pilgrims' Progress: A Story of the City Beautiful (1895) fulfilled a commission to turn a description of the 1893 Chicago Columbian Exposition into a book for children. Foreshadowing the journey of two boys across Europe in her later adventure romance, *The Lost Prince,* Burnett portrays twelve-year-old twin orphans traveling alone to the fair, after they have earned money for their train fare by working for their aunt on her Illinois farm. As Francis J. Molson has pointed out,[12] Burnett secularizes John Bunyan's Christian allegory by celebrating the American work ethic and defining heaven as the technological and material fruits of American ingenuity and energy, symbolized by the exposition. However, through her portrayal of the children's aunt, concerned only with the success of her farm and her growing bank account, Burnett shows that devotion to work alone shrivels the imagination and keeps one from enjoying many of life's pleasures. Also, Burnett cannot resist giving the story her usual fairy-tale ending, suggesting that achieving the Amercan dream requires a little luck as well as industry. At the fair, the children meet an embittered wealthy man who has just lost his wife and child; he gains new interest in life from his company with the children and adopts them. In its fairy-tale plot and its ending—children's beneficent effect on an adult and a newly created family—*Two Little Pilgrims' Progress* resembles Burnett's better-known children's books; unlike them, however, it maintains primarily an historical interest.

The One I Knew the Best of All

Burnett's childhood memoir, *The One I Knew the Best of All*, began as a sketch for inclusion in *Giovanni and the Other*. It grew too long to be included, however, and Burnett decided it was not appropriate for a collection intended primarily for children. The memoir "belongs to the grown-ups—especially those who are interested in children as a sort of phsycological [*sic*] study,"[13] she told her editor, who in 1893 serialized it in *Scribner's* before publishing it as a book the same year. The narrative point of view is that of Burnett as an adult, who uses the third person to refer to herself as a child. At times, the winks and smiles of the adult narrator over the head of "the Small Person" are too obviously intended to manipulate the reader, but for the most part the two points of view are effectively contrasted, as they are in Kenneth Grahame's later, more famous evocation of his childhood, *The Golden Age* (1895). In many parts, Burnett succeeds in her aim of depicting "A Memory of the Mind of a Child," the subtitle given the memoir in its American edition. Burnett's ability to remember how the world appears to a child would be put to good use later in *A Little Princess* and *The Secret Garden*—*Little Lord Fauntleroy*, more like the memoir, maintains a smiling point of view somewhere above the head of its winsome hero.

Burnett's explorations of how her mind worked as a child form some of her memoir's most interesting passages. For example, she describes with some poignance her frustrations when, as a very young child, her lack of language facility caused adults to misunderstand and underrate her. Similarly, she portrays her growing realization that adults will sometimes take advantage of her trusting nature. She was horrified, for example, lest her small body slip through huge gaps in a park bench after a wry policeman told her that he would have to arrest her for trespassing on the grass even if she did not intend to (chap. 1). Burnett also depicts several stages in her perception of death. When she was four, she was too young to find much interest in the details of her father's death; at this stage, death was a "mystery of which there was so little explanation that it was not terrible"; it was "an idea too vague to grasp" (chap. 1). Several years later when death touched children like herself, however, she was ready to be curious about the dead bodies and to ask questions about the causes and meaning of this "Strange Thing" (chap. 10). Despite such scenes and questioning, Burnett's handling of death in her memoir is far less morbid and sentimental than in the stories about the deaths of children in *Giovanni and the Other*.

In the memoir, Burnett adds to her childhood reaction to death a more philosophic encounter during her adolescence in Tennessee. With Walt Whitman's "Out of the Cradle Endlessly Rocking" (1860) perhaps in mind, Burnett describes her inchoate longings as she daily watched a pair of doves who become separated. She would lie on the ground in a thicket she called her "Bower," and as she looked into the sky she felt that her soul was a bird broken loose from her body and hovering above it attached by a slender cord. She wondered what would happen if the cord broke: "Nobody would know that I had only died because I was so happy that my soul broke the chain" (chap. 14). This speculation about the soul's relation to the body as well as about the power of the individual mind to participate in the larger mind that controls the universe would become more explicit in several tales of the supernatural as well as other fiction after the turn of the century.

If Burnett's memoir owes something to Whitman, it owes much more to Wordsworth, whose portraits of the child in *The Prelude* (1805, 1850) and *Ode: Intimations of Immortality From Recollections of Early Childhood* (1807) directly or indirectly influenced many literary portrayals of the child in the nineteenth century. Like Wordsworth's, Burnett's—and Kenneth Grahame's—concept of the ideal childhood is one lived close to nature; *The One I Knew the Best of All* is Burnett's fullest early exploration of the pastoral themes which would enrich her finest book for children, *The Secret Garden*.

Besides the Tennessee "Bower," several other experiences with nature figure prominently in the memoir. Perhaps recalling how the austere mountains appealed to the boy Wordsworth's conscience after he stole a shepherd's boat in *The Prelude*, young Burnett finds that her having taken a candy she could not pay for spoils her enjoyment of "the Back Garden of Eden," the garden of an estate where she played (chap. 3). She nevertheless grieved the loss of this exposure to nature when her family moved to an urban dwelling near the smoking chimneys of the Manchester mills. Burnett stresses the imprisonment she felt there when the smutty rain often kept her indoors. In a scene previewing Burnett's use of a locked garden in *The Secret Garden,* Burnett describes her delight in finding unlocked the gate to an abandoned house, where she used her imagination to turn one tiny flower into mounds of roses, violets, and hyacinths (chap. 15). Burnett's adolescent enjoyment of the Tennessee mountains and thickets is described in a long chapter, "Dryad Days" (chap. 15); this chapter also foreshadows *The Secret Garden* through its rhapsodies about the changing seasons.

Other parts of this paean to nature underscore the fact that Burnett's memoir, like Wordsworth's *Prelude,* is a portrait of the artist as a child; or, as she put it, an account of how she "spent her early years in unconscious training, which later enabled her to make an honest livelihood" with her pen (chap. 12). Appropriately, therefore, the memoir ends with a narrative of how she sold her first story. Earlier, she had described how she had used fictional formulas to tell stories to her friends and to write others which she shared with her mother. Later, during her "Dryad Days" in Tennessee, Burnett suggests that nature was her prime tutor as a budding artist, as it had been for young Wordsworth and Whitman. Burnett stresses that the stories she had written in that "great murky, slaving, manufacturing town," Manchester (chap. 14), had been informed by epithets and formulas from magazine fiction and thus were highly artificial. In the Tennessee woods, however, she ceased "to 'pretend' in the old way" because there were "real things enough." Conventional descriptions of her heroine's physical attractions now "seemed less satisfying and less necessary." In her stories she "began to deal with emotions . . . and forests and Autumn leaves assisted them and seemed part of them somehow, as she was part of the forests themselves. In the [Manchester] Square she had imagined—in the forests she began to feel" (chap. 14). In *The One I Knew the Best Of All*—as in *Through One Administration,* which also had a firm biographical base—Burnett's own feeling managed to break through the literary conventions which sometimes shackled her imagination and dated the written results. The memoir belongs in a tier of about a half-dozen of longer works which top Burnett's literary achievement.

Transitional Love Romances

The Fortunes of Philippa Fairfax (serialized in 1886, published as a
book in 1888), *A Woman's Will* or *Miss Defarge* (1887), and *The Pretty
Sister of José* (1889) form a bridge between Burnett's early love stories
for *Peterson's* and the longer love romance, *A Lady of Quality* (1896);
these short, transitional works reflect the changes the conventional
romantic heroine had undergone during the hiatus in Burnett's practice of the genre.

The scrupulously conscientious heroine of *The Fortunes of Philippa
Fairfax* makes it very much a throwback to the earlier era, and it
merits little attention because it is such a spiritless reworking of the
old conventions: A poor young woman from London visits a distantly
related dowager in Scotland and wins the heart of the wealthy
woman's young heir. In 1889, it was turned into a play, *Phyllis,* as
was *The Pretty Sister of José* in 1903. It is possible that Burnett had
play production in mind when she wrote these romances and that her
experience in the theater during this period encouraged the tendency
toward melodrama in her fiction.

Melodramatic influences, as well as more assertive heroines such as
those in Burnett's other love romances of this period, were coming
from popular fiction as well as drama. Dring the 1860s, the sensation
fiction of writers such as Charles Reade, Wilkie Collins, Mary Elizabeth Braddon, and Mrs. Henry Wood did much to change the conventional ways in which romantic heroines would be portrayed. In
sensation fiction, rife with intrigue and crime, the formerly pure and
passive romantic heroine took on some of the traits of the melodramatic villain. In 1887, Burnett read many of Braddon's books,
among them almost certainly the most famous, *Lady Audley's Secret*
(1862).[14] Its plot is echoed in Burnett's *A Lady of Quality,* as will be
shown later, but the assertiveness of its heroine appears also in *The
Pretty Sister of José* and *A Woman's Will.* Braddon's young woman is
deserted by her husband, changes her identity, marries another man,
pushes her first husband down a well when he returns, and then covers up her crime. Recent critics such as Elaine Showalter and Winifred Hughes see *Lady Audley's Secret* as a "witty inversion of Victorian
sentimental and domestic conventions," to use Showalter's words.
"The dangerous woman is not the rebel or the bluestocking, but the
'pretty little girl' whose indoctrination in the female role has taught
her secrecy and deceitfulness." Outwardly conforming to the senti-

mental ideal of the fragile, blue-eyed blonde who is kind to everyone, Lady Audley "is particularly dangerous because she looks so innocent."[15]

Lady Audley's hiding of her strength and deviant behavior under an ultrafeminine exterior suggests the combination of traits Burnett herself exhibited. In "How Fauntleroy Occurred," Burnett did ally herself with progressive forces by having Vivian declare himself a supporter of female suffrage; but she usually avoided being cast as a "new woman," and among her intimates her fondness for dressing as "a pretty little girl" earned her the nickname, "Fluffy." However, the name was "only externally and superficially . . . appropriate," as her son Vivian avowed.[16] A Scribner's agent, who came to bargain about *Little Saint Elizabeth,* found Burnett attired as an invalid but "always 'on the make.' "[17] In her popular fiction as well as in her person, Burnett often adopted the strategy for simultaneously portraying traditional and nontraditional female roles used in *Lady Audley's Secret.* Through the heroine, the reader can experience the new or even the forbidden but feel safe knowing that it will eventually be checked by the expected literary conventions or by conventional explanations. Lady Audley's husband somehow manages to escape his fall, and so she turns out to be innocent of the act if not the impulse to murder; when she is finally unmasked, her deviant behavior is explained as the result of insanity.

The heroines of *The Pretty Sister of José* and *A Woman's Will* commit no crimes such as bigamy or attempted murder, but they do share Lady Audley's manipulative power and proud will. In *The Pretty Sister of José,* a Spanish coquette vows she will never marry. In Pepita's eyes, marriage means a loss of power; she looks at other women from her poverty-stricken neighborhood and sees them grow old quickly as they bear children and slave for their husbands only to find themselves rejected for younger women. And so, Pepita holds on to her power as a coquette and collects many victims for whom she has little pity. As later in *A Lady of Quality,* Burnett enhances her heroine's prodigious power with references to the supernatural. Pepita decides that her power over men derives not from her beauty but from something she cannot understand but suspects it may be "the Evil One."[18] When one of her cast-off suitors tells her "You are not a woman; you are a witch," she defiantly accepts and repeats this appellation (14).

Pepita does fall in love with a famous bullfighter, however, and when her proud demeanor drives him away, she changes her allegiance from the demonic to the divine in two female manifestations in order to get him back. Consultation with the moon goddess is suggested by scenes in which Pepita sings in the moonlight and waits for her lover. This female deity and passivity prove inadequate, however, and so Pepita begins praying regularly to the Virgin. Joining the side of the angels does not diminish her pride in her own power, however, for she now apparently believes she can manipulate the deity to get the bullfighter back as she had earlier used "the Evil One" to destroy men. On the last page of the story, Pepita explains her bullfighter's eventual return thus: "They always give me my way. I have always had it—the Virgin herself has given it to me" (127).

Of the three transitional romances, *A Woman's Will* or *Miss Defarge* is most skillfully executed and anticipates the plot of *The Shuttle,* as Thwaite notes.[19] Burnett's portrayal of ancient British families and their modern heirs in these romances may have been influenced by Charlotte Yonge's *The Heir of Redclyffe* (1853).[20] The plot of *A Woman's Will*—a French governess's will holds sway over the members of an aristocratic family—also resembles a more sensational story Louisa May Alcott had published in 1866 under the pseudonym A. M. Barnard. There is no evidence Burnett read Alcott's "Behind a Mask, or a Woman's Power," but the similar titles and themes of the two stories serve as reminders that a female author besides Burnett had written stories pushing at the conventional boundaries of female power while also writing children's books idealizing mothers.

The appeal of Burnett's short romance lies partly in her portrayal of the governess's use of her "woman's will." Miss Defarge is not satisfied with simply making the young heir fall in love with her. First, she must use a whip to turn her savage young pupils into her adorers, attend to the neglected business affairs of the estate, and bolster the self-respect of the lady of the manor who has been rendered spineless by the bullying of her carousing husband. Burnett's portrayal of the "modern" romantic heroine is enhanced also by two contrasting female types, the daughters of the local clergyman. Barbara is the conventional unmarried woman devoted to religious charities and Elizabeth is an easygoing, sumptuously endowed nature goddess, who reflects the seasonal cycle as she ambles through the meadows trailing white gauzy dresses in summer and purple velvet robes in winter. Both the self-denying religious devotee and the sensuous goddess are suggested to be out of date compared to the modern managing woman, Miss Defarge. All of Elizabeth's clothes are out of style, and Miss Defarge departs from Barbara's self-sacrificing attitude by pointedly not nursing her lover back to health after his gunshot wound. The theme of sex-role experimentation is suggested also by a comment Elizabeth makes to the scrupulous Barbara, who calls one of Elizabeth's uninhibited frolics "insane." "Really insane, now Barbara," Elizabeth replies, "like that stout, red, old Mr. Cushing, who thought he was a young lady of seventeen and insisted that he should have his waist laced in, and wear low-necked gauze dresses?"[21] Burnett does not pick up this theme of transvestitism elsewhere in this story; however, having her heroine adopt male manners and dress would be one of the primary means through which Burnett would argue for an expanding of female roles in her next romance, *A Lady of Quality*.

A Lady of Quality and *His Grace of Osmonde*

A Lady of Quality bears many resemblances to Braddon's *Lady Audley's Secret*. Like Lady Audley, Burnett's Clorinda Wildairs has a dual identity; however, since Clorinda's identities are defined as male and female and flaunted openly from the beginning, Burnett's story makes more direct assault on traditional female roles than did Braddon's. Born with the fiery temper of her father rather than the abject submissiveness of her mother, Clorinda tyrannizes the house servants and stable grooms who rear her before her father uses her—much like his favorite fighting cock—to entertain himself and his carousing cronies. For the first fifteen years of her life, Clorinda is a boy among men: She curses, sings ribald songs, rides her father's dangerous horse, and almost always wears brilliant male garb. On her fifteenth birthday, Clorinda rejects her male manner and attire for female modesty: At the stroke of midnight she appears before her comrades in rich brocades over hooped petticoats. After a successful career as an imperious coquette, she marries the wealthiest earl in the neighborhood and, faithful to her bargain with the old man, makes him a model wife. After he dies, she marries the duke of Osmonde, a young man of impeccable morals, blue blood, wealth, and influence; her life as his regal consort, as a loving mother, as a lady devoted to charities earns her the epitaph, when she dies, as "the purest and noblest lady God e'er loved."[22]

Like Lady Audley, Burnett's pure and noble lady has several potentially damning secrets. Before her marriage to the old earl of Dun-

stanwolde, Clorinda had given her love and probably her body to a
degenerate fop, Sir John Oxon. After she is engaged to the duke of
Osmonde, Oxon threatens to reveal his earlier affair with her. Much
as Lady Audley had impulsively pushed her inconvenient first husband down a well, Clorinda in a fury strikes Oxon on the head with
her loaded riding whip. Burnett proves more indulgent of her heroine's murderous impulses and deceptions than did Braddon, however.
Clorinda's anger does kill, and she manages to keep Oxon's death a
secret; far from being incarcerated in an insane asylum as Lady
Audley had been, Burnett's openly deviant and successfully deceptive
lady is granted all the happiness any Cinderella could wish with her
prince charming.

Not surprisingly, contemporary reviewers found *A Lady of Quality*
"unquestionably striking" but claimed that Clorinda's escape from
punishment represented a grievous breach of poetic justice.[23] The *Nation* reviewer was forced to "the amazing conclusion that Mrs. Burnett
is not conscious of having exposed vice" and he feared a "deluge of
publications from lady novelists all solemnly declaring that, in order
to live long and happily, . . . it is quite imperative for a woman to
commit every sin in the decalogue."[24] Such critics apparently did not
find Clorinda's deviant behavior to be convincingly brought into line
by the conventions Burnett had used in earlier magazine fiction to
show how willful heroines gradually accepted customary female roles:
being softened by a devoted, fatherly husband—Dunstanwolde; being
inspired by a saintly woman—Clorinda's sister, Anne; and finally
being overwhelmed by love when she meets her soul mate—the duke
of Osmonde. Setting the romance in the past—Clorinda is born in
1685—did not make its heroine more credible or palatable. The critics sneered at Burnett's imitation of eighteenth-century style and presentation of the romance, through its subtitle, as "a most curious,
hitherto unknown history, as related to Mr. Isaac Bickerstaff but not
presented to the World of Fashion through the pages of *The Tatler,*
and now for the first time written down."

For a twentieth-century critic, *A Lady of Quality* remains in many
ways a daring book, even if it is difficult to be sure exactly how much
of its rebelliousness was conscious on Burnett's part. Burnett's bor-
rowings from eighteenth-century literature and her having Clorinda
transform herself into a woman in 1700 as the new century dawns,
for example, suggest that Burnett intended a revision of the passive
eighteenth-century heroine, as described by authors such as Richard-

son and Pope. Clorinda's lover, Oxon, is once compared to Richardson's demonic seducer Lovelace in *Clarissa;* but Burnett's heroine proves anything but a saint who prays for help from her bed. Burnett also provides a gloss on Pope's mock-heroic poem, *The Rape of the Lock.* Oxon has as evidence that he had been intimate with Clorinda a five-foot strand of her hair he had cut without her knowledge. In Pope's poem, Belinda's similarly stolen lock of hair rises into the firmament as a star, but Burnett's Clorinda burns the evidence of her "rape" and becomes herself the star of her husband's social world and the heaven of their love. The humor of the generous sprinkling of words such as "mayhap," "ifackens," and "ods bodikens" may have been unintentional, as contemporary critics imply, but one suspects that Burnett smiled at her presumption in naming "Mr. Addison and Mr. Steele, Dr. Swift and Mr. Pope" (312) among the luminaries who paid homage to her "lady of quality."

As daring as Burnett's impiety toward eighteenth-century literary classics is her assault on nineteenth-century feminine ideals. An appropriate appraisal of the rebellion implied by Burnett's heroine, however, necessitates the reminder that other women writers of the time, such as Sarah Grand in *The Heavenly Twins* (1893), similarly portrayed female characters adopting male manners and dress; in addition, it should be recalled, Alcott's Jo in *Little Women* always played male roles in family theatricals. Usually, as in Burnett's case, this motif represents not a transvestite or lesbian impulse,[25] but a desire of the female writer to imagine what life would be like untrammelled by skirts and traditional female roles; the motif sometimes argued further that more "male" attributes should be accepted in women.

When Clorinda changes from a male childhood to a female adulthood, she takes with her two important powers she had learned as a male—the ability to ride the wildest of horses and to wield a whip too heavy for most women. Just before she kills Oxon with her riding whip, Clorinda chooses a horse that had killed two men and trains him to carry her majestically through Hyde Park. As her earlier ability to ride her father's horse, "Rake," symbolized Clorinda's ability to tyrannize her father, her current victory over the horse "Devil" shows her ability to overcome Oxon—his name indicates that he is a beast as well as a devil and a rake. The scenes describing Oxon's death and Clorinda's ability to keep it a secret show that the horse "Devil" is also intended to symbolize Clorinda's own fury. She temporarily loses control of this fury, and it kills Oxon; but she then controls her anger at fate's attempt to undo her and remains calm as she sits on a divan hiding Oxon's corpse while she entertains her usual afternoon guests.

Clorinda's escape from punishment for Oxon's death—and perhaps also for her defiance of traditional female roles—no doubt explains why contemporary reviewers saw in A *Lady of Quality* a gross breach of poetic justice. Poetic justice is served, however, if one sees as the villain of the piece not Clorinda but rather the excessive and brutal power of men over women, as personified not only by Oxon but also Clorinda's father. Against this villain, Clorinda rides forth as a divinely sanctioned female avenger. Among the superlatives Clorinda collects as she gallops through the romance are the names of several goddesses; most frequently and appropriately, she is compared to Diana and called the "queen of the hunting field" (151). After Oxon's death, she hunts for the women Oxon has ruined and helps them begin a new life.

Clorinda also becomes the witness, if not the agent, of punishment meted to her father for his insensitive if not brutal treatment of her mother Daphne as well as of Clorinda herself. The romance's opening scenes dramatize Wildairs's abuse and neglect of his wife. Disgusted that she has born only girls and has lost her beauty in the process, Wildairs leaves her to bear her ninth "whelp" alone, in an abandoned corner of the estate. Daphne sees that newborn Clorinda, unlike her previous daughters, is pretty; remembering how her own beauty had led to ruinous abuse and neglect from her husband, Daphne tries to smother the infant. Baby Clorinda has prodigious strength as well as beauty, however, and struggles free; when they are finally found, the dead mother's hand rests on the feet of the bawling child. Later, Clorinda's beauty does cause her to be exploited by her father, when he parades her before his cronies; Burnett's descriptions of how the "wine-shot" eyes of the old men oggle the fifteen-year-old Clorinda's legs in tight breeches stop just short of being pornographic (47).

Burnett insists that it is male rather than female guilt which deserves punishment in A *Lady of Quality* by her adaptation of a motif from Shakespeare's *Macbeth* in her portrayal of Wildairs's death. Macbeth's guilt, it will be recalled, causes him to be haunted by the ghost of the man he has murdered. Burnett's exculpation of Clorinda for Oxon's death and her desire instead to show erring males punished leads her to have not Clorinda but Clorinda's father envision the decaying corpse of Oxon, as he dies in a fit of delirium tremens; restrained by the strong arms of Clorinda, Wildairs dies confessing his guilt for mistreating his wife.

In her own ponderings about her guilt in Oxon's death, Clorinda sometimes impugns the God who gave her a furious temper and a father who encouraged it—an *Atlantic* reviewer pointed out the similarity to Thomas Hardy's blaming the "President of the Immortals" for Tess of the D'Urbervilles's murder of her lover.[26] Clorinda's innocence is given supernatural sanction also by a vision of her dead mother. Just before Clorinda's saintly sister Anne dies, she tells Clorinda that she had known of Clorinda's indiscretions with Oxon and the manner of his death, and that she had conspired with Clorinda to keep these facts secret. As she lies on the brink of death, however, Anne sees their mother in heaven who tells her she has done "no wrong" (350). By implication, Clorinda herself has done "no wrong"; as the efficient but not ultimate cause of Oxon's death and as the witness of her father's, Clorinda is the agent of female justice and can therefore go unpunished.

This reading of *A Lady of Quality* explains some, but not all, of this often incoherent, if "unquestionably striking," romance; as in *Through One Administration,* her earlier, realist exploration of female roles, Burnett was not in complete control of her material. The sensationalism in *A Lady of Quality* is unusual for Burnett, but its heroine is not eccentric, as it often appeared to readers who thought of Burnett primarily as the mother of *Little Lord Fauntleroy*. Burnett herself recognized the key place her "lady of quality" had in her oeuvre: "Clorinda is not at all a new departure for me—notwithstanding a certain misleading gentleness of literary exterior I have hitherto presented to the world. 'That Lass o' Lowrie's' was Clorinda in disguise—so were Rachel Ffrench and Christian Murdock in 'Haworth's.' So was Bertha Amory, who laughed and wore tinkling ornaments and brilliant symphonies in red when she was passing through the gates of hell—so was little Sara Crewe when she starved in her garret and was a princess disdaining speech."[27]

Burnett went on to describe the autobiographical basis for this type: "She represents what I have cared for most all my life—from the time that an insensate person in authority struck me across the upper part of my arm with a riding whip, and I lifted the frill of my short sleeve, and after regarding the livid cut on the soft flesh for a moment or so, looked up at the person who had done it and laughed. It was a brief little laugh, and I suppose I must have looked like the devil. Clorinda, you observe, has been in the immediate vicinity for some years, and traces of her are sure to be detected in more places than one."[28] Burnett would never again depict such an iconoclastic woman as Clorinda Wildairs, but "traces of her" are indeed to be found in the heroines of *A Little Princess, The Shuttle,* and *The Secret Garden,* as well as in minor characters in some of her other later romances.

Contemporary critics who saw *A Lady of Quality* as a cynical pandering to popular taste for the sensational were confirmed in this belief by *His Grace of Osmonde,* which Burnett dashed off to be available when *A Lady of Quality* opened as a play. Much of this second romance does sound like a tabloid article containing gossip about current celebrities. As the story of Osmonde's life before his marriage to Clorinda, the sequel embroiders the portrait of the ideal romantic hero begun in the earlier book—a man who combines the chivalric virtues with a willingness to unite with a powerful woman in an egalitarian marriage. *His Grace of Osmonde* also answers some criticisms of *A Lady of Quality* by stressing the genuineness of Clorinda's virtue as a woman as well as its seeds in her earlier life as a male. Adding no important themes but rather underscoring some from the earlier romance, *His Grace of Osmonde* has little interest on its own.

In Connection with The De Willoughby Claim

Burnett began writing *In Connection with The De Willoughby Claim* in 1880 but was not able to complete it until almost 1899, when it was published. No doubt her difficulties arose from its treatment of experiences she had largely put behind her; it portrays American scenes she had known before *Little Lord Fauntleroy* made her an international celebrity, and she was now increasingly turning her gaze toward Europe in her life and fiction. Though limited to America, *In Connection with The De Willoughby Claim* contains the most detailed and panoramic portrayal of society in her fiction. Taking place immediately before and after the Civil War, it takes the reader to a seat of the old aristocracy and a mountain village in the South; to a center of middle-class respectability and a milltown in New England; and, finally, to the nation's capital, Washington, D.C. Using this crosssection of American society as her background, Burnett presents two interrelated plots, appropriately described as a fairy tale and a melodrama. *In Connection with The De Willoughby Claim* thus easily fits

Cawelti's description of the "social melodrama," "the combination of melodramatic structure and character with something that passes for a 'realistic' social or historical setting." Through her portrayal of America and the predicaments of her main characters at the beginning of the romance, Burnett conveys the realist's sense of the world's frequent "injustice and disorder"; through her manipulation of popular plot conventions, Burnett brings the romance to a satisfying conclusion that affirms "a benevolent moral order in the universe."[29]

In this as in her later romances, Burnett shows that she was conscious of combining the two main streams of her earlier fiction. With great frequency she has her main characters marvel that in this "real" world they find themselves taking part in a fairy tale or a melodrama; and Burnett's reasons for combining realism with popular formula are suggested by the narrator of *In Connection with The De Willoughby Claim:* "The further from romance the world drifts, the fairer it becomes in its fagged eyes."[30] In justice to Burnett, one cannot attribute her decision to write romances after *Little Lord Fauntleroy* solely to a desire to make money. She was genuinely the "Romantick Lady" she called herself, and she did not like to see romance in its many forms disappear from the world, inside or outside of fiction. Moreover, her decision no doubt grew also from the belief in the power of positive thinking she increasingly used to cope with her illnesses and other sorrows such as Lionel's death. Just before her own death, she told Vivian, "Long ago, even when I was a little girl writing in the attic room, . . . I began to feel that I could not have it on my conscience to make people unhappy, or make their minds foul with anything I had imagined or put on paper. . . . With the best that was in me I have tried to write more happiness into the world."[31] The undeniable craftsmanship and power of some of Burnett's later romances for children and adults argue a large measure of sincerity in this statement even if it may sound like rationalization for romantic escape to a critic who wishes Burnett had continued the more somber realist course suggested by *Through One Administration.*

The title of *In Connection with The De Willoughby Claim* alludes to its fairy-tale plot. Tom De Willoughby is a lumbering but sensitive son of Judge De Willoughby in Tennessee; ill-suited to a gentleman's life, Tom goes to the mountains of North Carolina and sets up a store. He adopts a baby girl left to his charge by a mysterious gentleman from the North after the baby's mother dies in childbirth in a cabin nearby. Just before the war, coal is discovered on old Judge De

Willoughby's land in Tennessee; but the war interrupts his plans to mine it, and his Union sympathies in a secessionist county exacerbate his financial setbacks caused by the war. When he dies, the judge leaves his ruined estate to his grandson, Rupert, who manages to find Tom; together, they go to Washington to claim reparation for the De Willoughby estate's ruin during the war. Rupert and Tom's ward, Sheba, have an Arcadian courtship; like other pairs of lovers in Burnett's romances, they are compared to Adam and Eve and their story is called "Romeo and Juliet without the tragedy" (356). The De Willoughby claim excites the imagination of a Washington, D.C., jaded by the machinations of many not so "innocent" claimants; the two lovers and Tom win great wealth with their claim and live happily ever after.

Tragedy does touch Burnett's second, melodramatic plot. Through the story of Sheba's ancestors in New England, Burnett rewrites Nathaniel Hawthorne's *Scarlet Letter* (1850) with a more "modern" theology. The man who left Sheba with Tom was the brother of the unwed mother; overpowered by his Calvinist vision of a vengeful God, this ascetic clergyman, Lucien Latimer, is guilt-ridden because he fabricated a pretty story about his sister's death to cushion the blow for their mother. Sheba's unacknowledged father is a "modern" Arthur Dimmesdale, the Reverend John Baird. Baird wins national renown for sermons claiming that the God who uses eternal punishments and rewards to make people moral was the creation of an earlier stage of evolutionary humanity. For Baird, "Humanity," not some "abstract, far-off Deity," is the "awful reality" (320). In his most famous sermon, Baird says that "Repentance Is Not Enough," because it cannot undo wrongs committed; knowing that "the laws of nature" will cry out if he violates another, "each man" should "constitute himself a god—of justice, pity, and mercy—until the world's wounds are healed" (320, 334). Having transgressed, one should pray for pardon not to God but to the person he has wronged.

Like Hawthorne's Dimmesdale, John Baird delays what he knows he ought to do. He does not confess to Latimer that he had had an affair with Latimer's sister; rather, he encourages Latimer to become his intimate friend and "shadow." Through the detective work of one of Tom De Willoughby's acquaintances, Baird is unmasked just before giving his last, triumphal sermon in the nation's capital. When Latimer learns the truth, he shoots himself; unable to forgive himself for having loved his sister's seducer, he dies the victim of his theology based on guilt and a vengeful God. In contrast, Baird's theology of "justice, pity, and mercy" allows him to survive; he had listened to Latimer—Burnett's Chillingworth—give repeated accounts of how Sheba's mother feared eternal damnation in the last hours when she was "crucified" in childbirth (331). Baird declares that during these accounts he had been "crucified" himself (425); unable to undo the deaths of the poor Calvinists, Baird can help heal "the world's wounds" by becoming a second son to Latimer's mother and a friend of Sheba. The merciful Tom allows Baird to visit Sheba so long as he does not reveal that he is her father. And Burnett's final scene brings the plots of her fairy tale and her melodrama together in a happy ending which dramatizes the "benevolent moral order in the universe": As in *A Lady of Quality,* the sins of parents are not visited on their children. Sheba—often portrayed as a nature spirit like Hawthorne's Pearl—puts a wreath of "bridal blossoms" on her mother's grave; she lays her cheek on the ground, and whispers, "I am happy. Oh, do you hear? Do you hear?" (444–45).

By inviting the reader to compare her melodrama of adultery to *The Scarlet Letter,* Burnett does underscore certain tenets of the humanist replacement she posits for Puritan theism; unfortunately, the comparison to Hawthorne's exploration of the psychological and social effects of extramarital passion also calls attentions to depths of human experience that Burnett does not and perhaps could not plumb in the kind of romance she was writing. It would have been wiser to evoke the ghost of Dickens, one of the chief progenitors of the modern social melodrama. Burnett does not match the achievement of Dickens either, of course; but one of her primary excellences as a storyteller is her ability, like Dickens's, to bring many characters from different sectors of society into dramatic interaction, as in *In Connection with The De Willoughby Claim* and in her later long romances, *The Shuttle* and *T. Tembarom.*

Burnett's method of characterization is also similar to that of Dickens. As in *Little Lord Fauntleroy* and her later romances, Burnett sketches in the outlines of her characters soon after the reader meets them; her literary strategy is not so much to show change or development in these characters but to see how often she can present them entertainingly true to type in a variety of new situations. She especially succeeds with big Tom De Willoughby. Her light, humorous touch almost always keeps this "Herculean guardian angel" (56) from cloying. The reader laughs gently and uncondescendingly as the lumbering fellow seeks female advice about baby formula and frilly clothes; Tom's final acceptance of Baird as Sheba's "friend" is entirely credible, and his "claim" on the government and on his family fortune seems richly deserved.

This last work Burnett published during the nineteenth century elicited mixed reviews from contemporary critics, who were apparently now sure that she could make no claims as a serious novelist and had firmly joined the ranks of popular romancers. The *Nation* reviewer was pleased that Burnett had averted her gaze from the "British aristocracy, magificently depraved" in *A Lady of Quality,* and he acknowledged a "freshness and sincerity in the presentation of the De Willoughby ugly duckling." He declared the episodes concerning Reverend Baird "offensive," however, and hoped that "women novelists can be persuaded or coerced into suppressing something of what they know about adultery and seduction." The *Athenaeum* reviewer was more chivalrous, attributing the "things over-emphasized . . . to the female temperament"; he found the sketches of Southern life "entertaining" and the book on the whole "clear and easy," "decidedly pleasant reading."[32] Such condescension would mark most of the praise critics would give the romances Burnett wrote in the twentieth century.

Chapter Four

Fairy Stories for Children and Adults (1900–1924)

From 1900, when Burnett was fifty-one years old, until 1924, when she died at age seventy-four, she produced some of her best writing for children—*A Little Princess* (1905), *The Secret Garden* (1911), and, though a lesser achievement, *The Lost Prince* (1915)—as well as two long romances for adults still able to engage a sympathetic reader—*The Shuttle* (1907) and especially *T. Tembarom* (1913). The continuing energy that propelled Burnett through a long publishing career is further demonstrated during this period by experiments in a genre new to her, the occult tale—*In the Closed Room* (1904) and *The White People* (1917). For the most part, however, Burnett continued literary themes and techniques she had used in the nineteenth century, which accounts for the critics increasingly viewing her as a Victorian anachronism.

Burnett continued to explore roles for women, portrayed social relationships between Americans and the British, and offered critiques of traditional religious doctrines and concepts of God. Appearing increasingly in her fiction after the turn of the century were speculations about the interrelationship of mind and body growing out of her earlier amateur interest in theosophy and Christian Science. In some of Burnett's later romances she portrayed social and political upheavals in Europe caused by World War I, but, while trying to address these contemporary concerns of her twentieth-century audience, she expressed a strong nostalgia for the Victorian past.

With the exception of her tales of the occult, Burnett also used literary forms from her earlier career—fantasies for children, romances for children and adults. She continued to rely on the Cinderella tale, as she had done in many of her early love romances and *Little Lord Fauntleroy;* the first work she published in the new century was a modern setting of this tale for adults, *The Making of a Marchioness* (1901), and she soon followed it with another version of the Cinderella tale for children, *A Little Princess.* Because of their idealized portrayal of character and the "real" world and their manipulation of plot to create a happy ending, however, almost all of Burnett's fiction during the last phase of her career could be called "fairy stories"—especially if one accepts the broad definition Burnett had given at the end of *Two Little Pilgrim's Progress*: "There are beautiful things in the world, there are men and women and children with brave and gentle hearts. . . . There are birds in the sky and flowers in the woods, and Spring comes every year. And these are the fairy stories."[1]

Fantasies for Children

Burnett paid tribute to her fairy muse through a whimsical self-portrait in the first of a series of short fantasies she published in *St. Nicholas* between 1906 and 1909. The title character in "The Troubles of Queen Silver Bell" (October 1906) is a fairy who lost her temper and gained the name Queen Crosspatch when she learned that children are ceasing to believe in fairies. Probably taking her cue from James Barrie's popular play, *Peter Pan* (1904), in which Tinker Bell manipulates the child audience to confess a belief in fairies, Burnett has her Queen Crosspatch become an advocate for the fairies through a series of stories describing the fairy queen's activities in the lives of various children. As her "A-manu-en-sis," Queen Crosspatch uses "a *quite* Respectable Person" who sits in a garden and writes books for a living, obviously intended to be Burnett herself.[2] The tales Queen Crosspatch whispers in the author's ears are an odd assortment, once again demonstrating that Burnett's best talents in writing for children did not lie in fantasy. The silliest are "How Winnie Hatched the Little Rooks" (November 1906) and "The Cozy Lion" (February–March 1907). In the first, Queen Crosspatch makes a girl tiny enough to hatch the eggs in an abandoned nest and to act as a saucy wife to the proud father bird who returns. In the second tale, perhaps inspired by Kenneth Grahame's "The Reluctant Dragon" (1898), Queen Crosspatch helps a lion develop the social skills needed to join children's frolics. A bit too sweet is "The Spring Cleaning" (December 1908–January 1909) in which Queen Crosspatch and her minions hasten spring so that little "Bunch" can have a primrose party for her friends. The best of the series is "Racketty-Packetty House" (December 1906–January 1907), dramatized in 1912 by the Children's Theater in New York using a cast of children. Portraying a neglected but happy-go-lucky family of dolls in the dog-

eared Racketty-Packetty House and the high-society antics of a new
set of dolls in Tidy Castle, this tale borrows heavily from Burnett's
early popular romances for adults, especially *Vagabondia*.

In addition to this series for *St. Nicholas*, Burnett published two
plodding and didactic books probably derived from tales she com-
posed orally for her children, since they are episodic and contain narrative frames explaining that they were told to a little boy by his
mother. The title character of *The Good Wolf* (1908) takes a poor boy,
Barty, to a feast held by some animals. In the sequel, *Barty Crusoe
and His Man Saturday* (1909), the wolf takes Barty, who has just read
Robinson Crusoe, to a desert island where a monkey, Saturday, helps
him deal with the Polite Pirates and Impolite Pirates. Also containing a fantasy journey is Burnett's only picture book, *The Way to the
House of Santa Claus* (1916). Having the subtitle, *A Christmas Story for
Very Small Boys in Which Every Little Reader Is the Hero of a Big Adventure,* the book's text omits the name of the hero so that the reader's
name can be inserted. The story has a cumulative form, as a series of
animals guide the hero to Santa Claus's house. Because of the economy of the text and the colorful simplicity of the full-page pictures
by an anonymous illustrator, this book is more engaging than the
earlier Barty books.

By far the best of Burnett's efforts in fantasy is *The Land of the Blue
Flower* (1909), which, like the two Barty stories, appeared in Vivian
Burnett's *Children's Magazine* before being published as a book. *The
Land of the Blue Flower* is a moral fairy tale which recalls but does not
match in evocative power those written by George MacDonald. In
this tale Burnett touches on a theme from earlier works such as
Through One Administration and *A Lady of Quality*—overcoming strong
emotions such as anger; and it anticipates in several ways *The Secret
Garden*. As does the later *Lost Prince, The Land of the Blue Flower* depicts the education of a prince. Young prince Amor from the plains
is sent to the mountains to be educated by the Ancient One. There,
Amor learns that all nature's creatures are his brothers; even lions
fawn on him as they had "on young Adam in the Garden of Eden."³
The prince first experiences anger when a horse sent from the plains
refuses to do his bidding. Amor's puzzlement over this strange emo-
tion elicits from his tutor an explanation and prescription which im-
plies the relationship between thoughts and physical health which
Burnett would posit in *The Secret Garden*. "When a man is overcome
by anger he has a poisoned fever," the tutor says; "he loses his

strength, he loses his power over himself and over others" (26). The prescription for handling anger in this fantasy is quite different from that in *A Lady of Quality*, which had Clorinda use her forceful will to master her wild horses and anger. A more mellowed Burnett now has Amor's tutor suggest a diversionary strategy: "If you put into your mind a beautiful thought it will take the place of the evil one" (27).

Again anticipating *The Secret Garden, The Land of the Blue Flower* portrays the healing effects of gardening. On the mountain, Amor tends a neglected garden once owned by his ancestor, a sad young queen. Much as the abandoned garden of his mother would bring healing to young Colin in *The Secret Garden,* a blue flower from this dead queen's garden helps Amor transform his kingdom on the plains when he returns as king. Amor decrees that everyone grow a blue flower; this sharing of nature's magic and beauty, as well as Amor's reporting of his tutor's assertion that "there is no time for anger in the world" (26), brings peace to his strife-torn kingdom.

Religious and Occult Tales

The Land of the Blue Flower, A Secret Garden, and the works to be discussed in this section confirm Vivian Burnett's statement that Burnett had "a strong religious sense" though she was "never orthodox."[4] Born into the Church of England and a frequent reader of the Bible if not a churchgoer, Burnett used various intellectual and religious movements of her day in her individual search. *In Connection with The De Willoughby Claim* showed that scientific and especially Darwinian theories had caused her to question some traditionally Christian concepts of the deity and his relationship to human beings. Perhaps congruent with this humanistic turn in her thinking was Burnett's appreciation for the interrelationship of body and mind implicit in Christian Science. Burnett's willingness to question orthodox Christian interpretations of scripture and concepts of the deity also allowed Burnett to pursue alternate explanations for the mysteries of life and death, such as those in theosophy. The result was the eclectic faith evidenced in her fiction.[5]

Although Burnett sometimes used the image of the crucified Christ to intensify the suffering of her characters, as in *In Connection with The De Willoughby Claim,* she focused on the mystical power of Christ in only one of her works, *The Little Hunchback Zia* (1916). In this slight, sentimental tale, a Syrian outcast follows Mary and Joseph to Bethlehem and is healed of his leprosy and crippled body when the new-born Babe puts his hand on Zia's shoulder. Similarly sentimental in its portrayal of social outcasts is *The Dawn of a To-morrow* (1906), put on the stage in 1909 and 1910 and often credited, like *The Secret Garden,* as a "Christian Science book," according to Vivian Burnett.[6] In *The Dawn of a To-morrow,* a wealthy man with some never-named physical or mental illness is dissuaded from committing suicide by the faith and goodness displayed by some London beggars. The story not only affirms the power of positive thinking to cure physical and psychological ills but also offers an interpretation of God's role in human suffering congruent with the underlying philosophy of Christian Science. Burnett has a destitute, old, crippled woman take on the theological crux of an omnipotent deity's responsibility for evil: God "never done the accidents and the trouble. It was us as went out of the light into the dark. If we'd kep' in the light all the time, an' thought about it, an' talked about it, we'd never 'ad nothin' else." Congruent with the monistic philosophy of Christian Science, the humble theologian uses her imagery of light and darkness to deny the reality of evil: "Accidents and trouble" "ain't nothin' but the dark—an' the dark ain't nothin' but the light bein' away." Reflecting the Christian Science denial of the ultimate reality of the material or physical world, the destitute sage whispers in the ears of a dying woman, *"There is no death."*[7]

These doubts about the ultimate reality and finality of the material world—the belief that *"there is no death"*—inform two of Burnett's occult tales, *In the Closed Room* (1904) and *The White People* (1917). In these works, both much superior to *The Dawn of a To-morrow,* characters receive evidence that loved ones who have died remain close to them and happy in another form—Burnett had consoled herself with this belief after her son Lionel died in 1890. These tales of the occult, like the moral fairy tale, *The Land of the Blue Flower,* suggest the influence of George MacDonald. While Burnett had met him in 1873, her biographers do not indicate that she especially appreciated his works. The two authors' shared belief in a benevolent God, use of imagery of light and darkness to deny the reality of evil, and portrayal of a material world which yields to the superior claims of the spiritual world in an afterlife, may have resulted less from the direct influence of MacDonald on Burnett than from the fact that Christian Science, which demonstrably did influence her, was partially derived

from Emmanuel Swedenborg, who also inspired MacDonald's heter-
odox views.

MacDonald's influence on Burnett is supported, however, by some
formal as well as philosophical resemblances. *In the Closed Room* in
several ways recalls MacDonald's *At the Back of the North Wind*
(1871), for example. Like Macdonald's ethereal child Diamond, Burnett's Judith is born to laborers in London and frequently "falls
awake" into a flower-filled realm which seems more real than the
noisy elevated railroad and domestic quarrels outside her bedroom
window. When her parents become caretakers for a mansion while its
wealthy owners are away, Judith finds herself able to push open the
locked door to a fourth-floor room, where she plays wordlessly with
a little girl. As Macdonald's Diamond finally leaves his treehouse to
go permanently to the beautiful country at the back of the north
wind, Burnett's Judith and her friend eventually disappear along a
green path extending from the roof garden just outside the closed
room.

In this short tale, Burnett handles nicely the clues which gradually
reveal that Judith's mysterious playmate is the recently dead child
who had lived in the mansion. Burnett's stylistic economy yields to
sentimental excess only in portraying the grief of the wealthy mother,
who returns to be comforted when she sees that the girl's room has
been rearranged as it had been when she was alive; the mother knows
that the girl had wanted to show her that she is not far away. Wisely,
Burnett ends the story as the housekeeper recognizes that her Judith
is also dead; despite a minor lapse, Burnett handles maternal grief
more effectively than she had in the stories written shortly after Lionel's death. *In the Closed Room* anticipates *The Secret Garden* through
its mysterious locked room and its garden; but this short tale also has
an evocative power of its own.

The White People, dedicated to Lionel, also portrays a mother's
eventual consolation for the death of her son. In this case, however,
the son is an adult whose death is, until the end of the story, only
anticipated—he has an incurable heart defect. The story is narrated
by a young woman who falls in love with him. The solitary heir of
a noble family in Scotland, the narrator, Ysobel, has the gift of second sight, the ability to see pale, "white people," whom she later
learns have died. As a child, for example, she had sometimes played
on the moors with a child killed during a savage war during Scot-

land's remote past. Ysobel also has dreams in which she visits a lovely hillside which seems more real to her than the rest of her life. Ysobel's visions of the "white people" and her visits to the hillside help the young man and his mother lose their fear of death and separation from each other. At the end of the story, he dies and the narrator says that she has often seen him since, smiling at her.

The young man in *The White People* is a world famous author whose writings had given Ysobel a feeling of close companionship even before she met him. For the critic who sees the imprint of MacDonald on some of Burnett's fiction, it is tempting to see this author as her tribute to that Scotch writer. The fictional author's love of Scottish legends may also suggest Sir Walter Scott, whom Burnett claims to have loved as a child; but the author's name, Hector MacNairn, and the description of what he wrote, "essays and poems, and marvelous stories,"[8] even more recall MacDonald. Besides, Burnett's analysis of the strange occurrences in her story as well as her description of her tale's meaning echo MacDonald. As MacDonald had described the country at the back of the north wind as music in another key from that on earth, one of Burnett's characters conjectures that Ysobel's ears and eyes register "music" as well as "colors" from a "dimension" just beyond earthly perception (62).

As does MacDonald in his essay, "The Fantastic Imagination" (1893), Burnett suggests that because the human mind is part of the Mind which created it, it can learn to perceive more of that great Mind's workings. Accidents—such as Ysobel's meeting MacNairn, and the shipwreck in *At the Back of the North Wind*—are viewed as such only by those not yet able to perceive the great law which governs all. Near the end of her tale, Burnett makes a comment on its meaning which recalls MacDonald's description, in his essay, of the meaning of his fairy tales. "What does it matter if this seems a strange story?" Ysobel asks the reader. "To some it will mean something; to some it will mean nothing. To those it has a meaning for it will open wide windows into the light" (109).[9] Some readers may feel that Burnett's analysis of the occult events in *The White People* makes the tale too didactic, and prefer *In the Closed Room,* which omits such speculation; and Burnett's unraveling of her mystery through the narrative itself is not handled as subtly as in the earlier work—Burnett rarely used first-person narrative to advantage. However, both *In the Closed Room,* with its preternaturally transformed nursery and roof garden, and *The White People,* with its ghostly visitors on the Scottish moors, have the eerie atmosphere usually admired in fiction portraying alternate dimensions of human experience.

Burnett portrays another example of second sight as well as speculations about human evolution, elementary thought processes, and the artistic impulse, in a short tale for *St. Nicholas,* "The First Knife in the World" (December 1909). A psychically gifted boy from Scotland visits the British Museum, declares a knife on display to be the first one in the world, and goes into a trance during which he watches a prehistoric boy invent it. Like so many of Burnett's characters, this "Human Thing"[10] is different from his peers; here, as elsewhere in her fiction, Burnett suggests that the evolutionary process sometimes makes abrupt leaps forward through such natural leaders. Compared to his fellows, this boy is not so hairy, walks more often on two legs, makes more sounds, and is more observant of his surroundings. Until this stage in the evolutionary process, human beings had apparently perceived no difference between mind and body, for the boy has always treated any unhappiness as physical hunger. On this day, however, the boy utters a sound somehow related to a feeling of wanting something other than food. He plays with a stone and when, by accident, a piece falls off, he realizes he can make the stone narrower. He forgets his hunger and utters another, joyful sound, "I have made" (103). The boy's use of language proves to be a power; the animals around him are afraid because they have never heard sounds like these. Accidentally cutting his finger on the stone, the boy realizes he can use the stone to cut beasts. When he kills a wolf about to attack a baby, he has two more new thoughts. He realizes he has saved something—until now, he had protected only himself; and he realizes he is different from the beasts—he begins to walk erect consistently. He expresses his new self-consciousness through a chant: "I am Man. I made that which was not in the world before. I save as well as kill. I am Man" (105).

"The First Knife in the World" continues the exploration of elementary thought processes Burnett had begun in her memoir, subtitled *A Memory of the Mind of the Child.* Particularly interesting are Burnett's portrayal of the interrelated roles of the human body, the physical world, and language in the development of human consciousness. Moreover, by stressing the role of "making" in the boy's awakening consciousness, a making of something which can save as well as kill, Burnett may be suggesting the elemental nature of the artisic impulse and the great power for good and evil in what it makes. If so, this short tale for children represents perhaps the most sophisticated published statement Burnett made about her view of herself as an artist; it suggests her perception that the impulse to "make" was an integral part of her identity and of her decision to use her "making" to promote good—"to write more happiness into the world," as she told Vivian before she died.[11]

Longer Romances for Children and Adults

The intention to promote happiness is apparent in all of the longer romances for children and adults Burnett wrote from 1900 until her death in 1924. These romances will be discussed in their order of publication rather than grouped according to their intended audiences, since Burnett used many of the same themes, character types, and plot structures in writing for children and adults. Moreover, a chronological study of the romances of this period helps define the arc of Burnett's achievement. During the first fifteen years of the century, most of her romances maintain the imaginative energy of her earlier fiction, and they often exhibit excellent craftsmanship and a polished style. After about 1915, however, Burnett's style becomes increasingly flaccid; she repeats key ideas too often, and she shows a decreasing ability to breathe new life into the conventions she had earlier used with ingenious variety.

The Making of a Marchioness and *The Methods of Lady Walderhurst.* The first work Burnett published after the turn of the century was a contemporary setting for adults of the Cinderella tale, *The Making of a Marchioness* (1901). Critics were at a loss to explain its special charm. The *Athenaeum* reviewer, for example, caviled at its improbabilities but admitted that he nevertheless grew interested in the heroine's "works and ways (and even her skirts)." "Perhaps," the reviewer concluded patronizingly, "the author's numerous admirers will not be hypercritical but will enjoy her story without analyzing it."[12] *The Making of a Marchioness* does reward analysis, however, if one recognizes it as an exceedingly clever example of formula fiction, as described by John G. Cawelti, rather than a realist novel, as the *Athenaeum* reviewer seemed to assume.

The effectiveness of a particular work of popular, formula fiction, like that of a particular retelling of a familiar fairy tale, depends on the degree to which it intensifies the expected enjoyment of the formula by varying it, as Cawelti points out. Familiar character types may be revitalized by including some nontypical traits or by adding a few unexpected "touches of human complexity."[13] Similarly, realist touches may be added to the story's setting. Such variations of the formula not only alleviate the boredom caused by the totally familiar but also encourage reader identification with the main character and intensify suspense—by suggesting that this time the realist impulse will win out and the author will withhold the desired happy ending. At times, it may appear that the author is criticizing the formula, but the ultimate purpose is to revitalize and thus save it rather than reject it.[14]

In *The Making of a Marchioness,* Burnett cleverly plays all these games, and her description of the romance shortly after she finished it shows that she knew what she was doing. *The Making of a Marchioness* "is a study of a [character] type, and in an atmosphere [fashionable British society] I know so well," she said. "It is a picture of a nice, simple, sweet prosaic soul who arrives at a good fortune almost comic because it is . . . so incongrous. Its heroine is a sort of Cinderella . . . with big feet instead of little ones." "Emily Fox-Seton . . . is invited to a big country house because she can be made useful, and she trudges about waiting on everyone and being so sympathetic and interested in the various beauties who are 'stalking' the Marquis, who is such an abnormal catch—and he cooly proposes to her." "The cleverness of the thing (I know it is clever) lies in the studies of character and the way in which the most wildly romantic situation is made compatible with perfectly every-day and unromantic people and things. The Marquis of Walderhurst is totally unromantic and so is nice, *un*clever Emily Fox-Seton."[15]

Even a "hypercritical" "admirer" of *The Making of a Marchioness* can believe Burnett's sincerity when she said, "I can't tell you how I enjoyed writing it";[16] for its comic successes are matched in her fiction only by some scenes in the later *T. Tembarom,* about a male Cinderella, a grown-up version of Little Lord Fauntleroy. Particularly "clever" is the episode in which the marquis proposes to Emily Fox-Seton; as in the fairy tale, Burnett's Prince Charming proposes not at the "ball" but at the scene of his Cinderella's humble service. Like Charles Perrault in his witty versions of fairy tales, Burnett uses "every-day" details to laugh at the familiar formula even as she is enjoying it. After a day in which she has exhausted herself supervising a village treat given by her hostess, Emily must walk four miles to a village to get fresh fish for dinner. For the long walk on a hot day, Emily dons an unfashionable brown dress and loose slippers, since her already big feet are swollen from the previous day's labors. Despite such precautions and her hurry to get home in time, she finds that the intense heat, the strong smell of fish, and the blisters on her feet cause her to take occasional rests. It is in this "unromantic" situation that the marquis finds Emily and declares that her personality, if not her foot, is the right size for a wife: "I am a selfish man, and I want an unselfish woman."[17]

As suggested by the marquis's proposal, Burnett's portrayal of marriage is as "unromantic" as her heroine and hero. The marquis declares himself "not a marrying man," but he "must marry" (182) to gain an heir for his vast fortune. Women similarly marry more for social reasons than for love, as is shown by Emily's three competitors for the marquis. A wealthy young American woman and a lady writer seek a marriage to add luster to their already established social status. For Lady Agatha Slade as well as Emily Fox-Seton, however, marriage means social and possibly personal survival. Well-born Emily has no wealthy relatives to support her, and Lady Agatha has five younger sisters waiting for her to marry so that their poor father can afford to introduce them into society. This is Lady Agatha's last reign in the "illustrated papers"—"in these days a new beauty is advertised like a new soap," quips a worldly wise dowager (71). If Lady Agatha does not find a husband this season, she must yield her place to the next sister in line and return to the family castle in Ireland, a "Bastille" where she will waste as an old maid and "never get out alive" (72). By portraying high society as a merciless marriage market, Burnett couples her comic portrayal of her heroine with an often-satiric view of society, again following the precedent of Perrault.

By introducing comedy and social satire—as by adding touches of realism, as Cawelti notes—the writer of formula fiction is playing a dangerous game. Too much of such variation can criticize the formula too severely and thus undercut rather than intensify the satisfaction of the happy ending.[18] In *The Making of a Marchioness,* Burnett walks this precipice daringly but skillfully. Her light, comic tone controls her occasional touches of satire, and she manages her Cinderella's three rejected "sisters" so that they ultimately enhance the happy ending. The three women's use of money, wit, and phenomenal beauty to catch the marquis effectively highlight Emily's unselfishness and humility—she knows she has none of the other women's

qualities and it never occurs to her that she might be a contender for
the marquis's proposal. As a result, the proposal is almost as surprising and as satisfying to the reader as to Emily herself; when Lady
Agatha receives a proposal from another wealthy man, the fairy tale's
demands for poetic justice are doubly satisfied.

The Making of a Marchioness cannot claim to be Burnett's "best
novel," as is suggested by Marghanita Laski and Ann Thwaite.[19] Even
if one prefers the polish of Burnett's best adult romances to the uneven success of her more ambitious realist novel, *Through One Administration,* one must conclude that *The Making of a Marchioness* does not
have the thematic richness of her best child romances, *A Little Princess*
and especially *The Secret Garden.* It is, however, unquestionably Burnett's best love romance. *The Making of a Marchioness,* which Burnett
wrote in less than two weeks, is a *jeu d'esprit* by a writer justifiably
confident of her mastery of popular formula.

In *The Methods of Lady Walderhurst,* like its predecessor published
in 1901, Burnett depicts the early years of her Cinderella's marriage.
In portraying how the unsentimental marquis eventually falls in love
with the woman he had married for practical reasons, Burnett maintains some of the comic spirit of her earlier tale; she has some fun,
for example, with the marquis's unsentimental terms of endearment
in letters he writes Emily during a business trip. Burnett also continues her exploration of the kind of happiness available to the "unromantic," the "unclever," the "uncomplex"—the term used most
often in this sequel. "Only the brilliant logic and sensitiveness of genius really approaches knowledge of itself, and as a result it is usually
extremely unhappy," Burnett's narrator comments.[20] At the beginning of *The Methods of Lady Walderhurst,* lack of personal complexity
makes the marquis "never unhappy" and Lady Walderhurst the happy
worshipper of the husband she regards as a god who rescued her from
poverty. As the tale unfolds and Emily's devotion to her husband is
tested, however, the comic tone is overcome by the somber. Burnett's
Cinderella becomes a patient Griselda, the heroine of the "Clerk's
Tale" in Chaucer's *Canterbury Tales,* as Thwaite notes;[21] and Burnett
moves from fairy tale to melodrama—the two kinds of plot combined
in *In Connection with The De Willoughby Claim.*

Burnett's villain is the degenerate presumptive heir to Walderhurst's title and fortune, who contrives "accidents" to kill the pregnant Emily while her husband is away. Early in the tale, the young
man finds an ally in his Anglo-Indian wife and her Indian servant,

who practices the occult. The wife eventually defects from her husband's schemes, however, because her own pregnancy makes her susceptible to the unsuspecting generosity of the also-pregnant Emily. Because Emily does not want to burden Walderhurst, who has become ill during his travels, she does not tell him of her pregnancy and the threats on her life. Walderhurst returns just in time to call her back from the death she had risked so that their son could survive his difficult birth.

The Methods of Lady Walderhurst makes an interesting addition to Burnett's fictional exploration of female roles: Like *Through One Administration,* it portrays the dangers of exaggerated wifely devotion; and like the works of other female writers such as Mrs. Humphrey Ward, it depicts childbirth as an awesome rite bonding women otherwise set at odds. Moreover, its melodramatic story is effectively unfolded. Largely because it asks the reader to take its outdated conventions seriously rather than find them a source of comedy, however, *The Methods of Lady Walderhurst* does not maintain the appeal of *The Making of a Marchioness.*

A Little Princess. Although all three of Burnett's best-known child romances use themes and motifs from the Cinderella tale, *A Little Princess* (1905) shows this origin most clearly, perhaps because Burnett was working on it shortly after she published her Cinderella tale for adults, *The Making of a Marchioness,* in 1901. Burnett had made a preliminary sketch for *A Little Princess* in the short tale, "Sara Crewe" (1887–88); now, in 1902–3, her stage adaptation of that tale appeared in London and New York. When the play was declared an equal to that earlier based on *Little Lord Fauntleroy,* Scribner's asked Burnett to turn "Sara Crewe" into a longer work, incorporating the changes introduced in the play. Comparison of the resulting romance, *A Little Princess,* with *The Making of a Marchioness* and other previous adult works, as well as with its earlier versions as a short story and a play, demonstrate the integral relationship between her writing for adults and for children as well as the degree to which Burnett had grown as an artist since her first children's classic in 1886, *Little Lord Fauntleroy.*

More than *The Making of a Marchioness* and *Little Lord Fauntleroy,* *A Little Princess* remains faithful to the archetypal Cinderella tale. Many variants of the tale emphasize that the heroine is born a princess but is treated otherwise by a stepmother after her own mother dies. Cinderella's life as a servant thus represents an enchantment; she must be accepted by the prince in this state before she can return to her natural, disenchanted state as a princess.[22] Similarly, Sara Crewe in *A Little Princess*—though not in Burnett's earlier, story version—is regarded as a princess at the beginning. Her mother is dead, and her wealthy father brings her from India to a school in London, run by Miss Minchin, Sara's "wicked stepmother." For a time, all recognize Sara as a princess because of her rich clothes, intelligence, and kindness to the other pupils—her "step-sisters." Word arrives, however, that Sara's father has died penniless, and Miss Minchin instantly turns Sara into an ill-clad, half-starved servant. This "enchantment" is broken when the recluse next door recognizes Sara's true identity as a princess: He had been the business partner of Sara's father, had inherited all of the fortune the dead man mistakenly thought he had lost, and had been looking throughout Europe for Sara to restore her fortune to her. At the end of the romance, Sara makes her home with the recluse, where she entertains an extended family including the many child friends she has made.

A comparison of *A Little Princess* with *The Making of a Marchioness* shows how Burnett adapted her fairy-tale formulas for a child audience. As in *Little Lord Fauntleroy* and *A Secret Garden,* the happy ending in *A Little Princess* is represented not by getting married but by finding a family. In addition, in her child romances Burnett treats the fairy tale's usual coincidences and abrupt changes in fortune more as a cause for wonder than an occasion for comedy. This more serious tone in *A Little Princess* allows Burnett to meld melodrama—through Sara's interaction with Miss Minchin—into her fairy-tale plot, rather than keeping them separate as in *The Making of a Marchioness* and its sequel, and as in the two interlocked plots in *In Connection with The De Willoughby Claim.* This conflation of fairy tale and melodrama gives *A Little Princess* greater unity of tone than *In Connection with The De Willoughby Claim* and more richness of characterization and theme than *The Making of a Marchioness* and her first children's classic, *Little Lord Fauntleroy.*

By drawing on the heroines of some of her adult fiction and on her childhood memoir, Burnett gives complexity to the heroine of *A Little Princess* without making the reader question that she is indeed a "princess" and richly deserves her fairy-tale reward. Gracious self-control, for example, does not always come easily for Sara, who, if a "princess," is "not an angel" (chap. 6). Sara does remain publicly stoic in the face of disasters such as separation from her father and his later death—her pride keeps her from expressing her sorrow except privately; but she sometimes loses this self-control when faced by injustices caused by others, especially those in authority. Sara bursts into "passionate sobs" (chap. 15) before another child after Miss Minchin falsely accuses and then punishes the servant girl for stealing meat pies, for example; and she sometimes verbally defends herself against unjust statements made by Miss Minchin or an older, jealous student in the school. Most frequently, however, Sara wins a victory over the sadistic school mistress by refusing to show that she is angry or hurt. "When you will not fly into a passion people know that you are stronger than they are, because you are strong enough to hold in your rage, and they are not. . . . There's nothing so strong as rage, except what makes you hold it in." (chap. 10). Thus, like Clorinda Wildairs in *A Lady of Quality,* Sara Crewe uses self-control as a means of gaining power over others. In reconciling herself to a life as a mistreated servant, however, Sara relies on her imagination, making her a fictional sister to the child Burnett portrayed herself to be in her memoir. Like Burnett as a child, Sara borrows from books she has read to tell stories to her schoolmates and to turn her trials into a romantic adventure; her rat-infested garret room becomes a cell in the Bastille, for example, or the Count of Monte Cristo's dungeon.

Sara's spirit is undaunted during her trials also because she believes in magic, "the Magic that won't let those worst things *ever* happen" (chap. 15). In *A Little Princess,* magic becomes a metaphor for Sara's ability to see with the imagination—to regard an attic snack as a feast in a grand palace—as well as an explanation for the marvelous changes in Sara's life as she increasingly finds herself living in a fairy tale—as when luxurious furnishings mysteriously appear in her room, put there while she slept by the servant of the recluse next door. This symbolic use of magic is further enhanced by Burnett's contrasting portrayal of Miss Minchin. Unlike Sara and some of the children who are undeceived by Sara's "enchantment" as a servant, Miss Minchin lacks the imagination to see beyond external appearances. She thinks Sara can be changed from a princess to a beggar by simply changing her frocks; she regards scullery-maids as "not little girls" but "machines" for making fires (chap. 7); she looks at the soap dish and tissue paper used in Sara's "magic feast" and sees only "rubbish" (chap. 15). Lacking the magic of imagination, Miss Minchin is immune to its transforming power; the end of the romance finds her in total defeat—she has lost a star pupil in the again wealthy Sara—and she is unable to understand how it happened.

The mature craftsmanship of *A Little Princess* is further demonstrated by noting how Burnett was able to incorporate additions from its stage version to give the resulting romance more dramatic complexity than *Little Lord Fauntleroy*. In part, drama is heightened by Sara's interaction with Miss Minchin; their personalities and objectives conflict far more than do those of Little Lord Fauntleroy and his irascible grandfather. In addition, and unlike Little Lord Fauntleroy, Sara has significant relationships with other children, a contribution made to the romance from the play. In the original tale, "Sara Crewe," only one of the children at the school was individualized—the plump, good natured but slow-learning Ermengarde. Probably to make the play more appealing for its intended audience of children, Burnett developed more of Sara's classmates, especially the jealous, older Lavinia, and the fretful toddler, Lottie; she also expanded her portrayal of a large family of children who visit the recluse next door, and she gave a prominent role to the servant Becky. By including and developing all of these children in her romance, Burnett skillfully manages more individualized characters than in any of her previous works for children. *A Little Princess* also exceeds them in its style. Burnett believed that young readers love the specific, and in this child romance she provided a wealth of concrete detail well-chosen to reveal character or create a mood—the angular furniture in Miss Minchin's school, for example, and the actual and imagined details of Sara's magic feast in the attic. *A Little Princess* does not have the lyric style and mythic imagery of *The Secret Garden,* but as a sustained performance of what it sets out to do, *A Little Princess* is second only to that later classic among her children's works and is exceeded by few if any of her adult works.

The Shuttle. *The Shuttle,* serialized in the *Century* beginning in 1906 and published as a book in 1907, is a social melodrama like Burnett's last long romance for adults eight years earlier, *In Connection with The De Willoughby Claim.* As in that work, Burnett interweaves two plots, a melodrama depicting the unhappy marriage of an American heiress to a titled British fortune hunter, and a fairy tale about her younger sister's courtship with an impoverished British nobleman. These formulaic plots are set against the background of the energetic business and social world of New York and the decaying country estates of once-powerful noble families in Britain. *The Shuttle* addresses several issues of contemporary interest Burnett was especially equipped to handle. The strong will and business acumen of its fairy-tale heroine portray expanding roles for women, especially American women—a theme from Burnett's earlier fiction. Through the older sister's suffering at the hands of a tyrannical husband, Burnett argues that wives should retain control of their own fortunes and that society should be more accepting of divorce. This melodramatic plot no doubt reflects Burnett's response to public criticism of her own divorce as well as her anger and frustration within her recent, second marriage to the temperamental British actor, Stephen Townesend.[23]

The overriding social theme of *The Shuttle,* however, is the melding of American and British societies through Anglo-American marriages and American tourism in England. The opening chapter describes "the great hand of Fate" weaving a "web" between the two countries;[24] the book's title, *The Shuttle,* alludes to the many steamers moving back and forth across the Atlantic—a crossing the Anglo-American Burnett would make thirty-three times during her lifetime. It was probably this social theme that made *The Shuttle* so popular— the royalties for the first three months of the American edition alone totaled $38,000, and the book entirely paid for the lavish home Burnett built at Plandome, Long Island, in 1909. By that year, according to Thwaite, over five hundred American women had married titled foreigners, taking with them some 220 million dollars. By giving her American family the name Vanderpoel, Burnett probably invited the reader to recall the celebrated marriage in 1895 of Consuela Vanderbilt to the ninth earl of Marlborough.[25] Burnett shared the popular dream of using wealth to recapture a romantic vision of Britain's aristocratic past, for from 1898 through 1907 she played lady of the manor at Maytham, a country estate she rented in Kent.

Perhaps because of the autobiographical basis for *The Shuttle,* as Thwaite suggests, Burnett found the book unusually difficult to write. She began it during the summer of 1900, just after she married Townesend, but she was not able to finish it until the fall of 1906, the year after she became an American citizen—to limit Townesend's claims on her fortune, Thwaite conjectures.[26] As she worked on *The Shuttle,* Burnett called it an " 'eadstrong" "D———,"[27] which fought her every inch of the way; and she gladly set it aside to write more enjoyable, "easy" books such as *The Making of a Marchio-*

ness and *A Little Princess*. Unfortunately, Burnett's "big" book does not have the surviving appeal of these "short, 'easy' " books.[28] The archetypal potential of the formula plots in *The Shuttle* is obscured by the amount of attention given social issues which have lost the appeal they had for the book's contemporary readers; as a result, it now seems repetitious and too long.

The Shuttle is not without historical interest, however. There is often an authentic ring to Burnett's portrayal of the business and family life of America's wealthy Four Hundred, of conditions on transatlantic steamers for common tourists as well as for the wealthy, and of the somewhat pathetic attempts of an impoverished British aristocracy to use American money to regain past social power and responsibility. Moreover, since the melodramatic and fairy-tale plots are more thoroughly integrated than in *In Connection with The De Willoughby Claim, The Shuttle* represents a structural advance over that earlier long romance. Its main character, the younger heiress, plays a more active role in both plots than does Tom De Willoughby. Bettina Vanderpoel comes to England to give psychological support to her unhappily married sister, and she uses the Vanderpoel money and her own extraordinary managerial skills to restore the decaying estate, entailed to her sister's son. While busy with these affairs, Bettina meets the last heir of Mount Dunstan. The two fall in love, but Dunstan's pride keeps him from expressing it—he does not want to appear a fortune hunter. The fairy-tale and melodramatic plots share the same climax when Dunstan intercepts the villainous husband's attempts to rape Bettina in an abandoned cottage—he wants revenge for Bettina's breaking of his tyranny over his wife. This scene marks the end of the husband's effective villainy, for soon after, he has a seizure, lapses into unconsicousness, and dies. The crisis in the cottage also overcomes the lovers' reticence so that they can declare their love. By the end of the romance, it is assumed that they will marry and that the Vanderpoel wealth will restore the Dunstan estate to its former glory.

Of the two plots in *The Shuttle,* the fairy-tale love story is considerably less effective. Burnett's excesses in describing her new "Adam and Eve" (324) recall her glorification of the noble couple in *His Grace of Osmonde,* the sequel to *A Lady of Quality*. The reader hears too much, for example, of the heroine's phenomenal grace and beauty and of the "Primeval Force" of the love she shares with the ambitious but pathetically fettered young Dunstan. Burnett further glorifies the lovers by presenting them as avatars of their ancestors, the Vanderpoel who established the family wealth in the fur trade—probably a reference to John Jacob Astor—and the medieval Dunstan remembered for his chivalry and prowess in war. Even acknowledging that Burnett intended this almost superhuman pair to symbolize the marriage between the best in American and British societies, the contemporary reader may find in this atavism a disquieting spector of Social Darwinism, with its positing of master races; also, some readers may not share Burnett's evident adulation of wealth and title.

The melodramatic plot in *The Shuttle,* on the other hand, is more effective, despite its similar exaggeration, primarily because of Burnett's often-clever presentation of the battle of wits and wills between Bettina and her sister's husband, Nigel Anstruthers, a battle in which Bettina proves a more self-possessed avatar of Clorinda Wildairs in *A Lady of Quality*. Like Clorinda, Bettina must use her wit, will, and money to overpower the villain without losing her reputation as a gracious lady. Bettina's task is further complicated because she fears an open battle with Nigel would upset the fragile psychological balance of her sister, who is just beginning to recover from her abject fear of her husband; Bettina must keep Nigel from using the weapon he has long held over his wife's head, a note which mistakenly suggests that she had an affair with a clergyman.

Like Bettina, Nigel is driven to covert tactics, since he does not want to cease benefitting, however indirectly, from Bettina's wealth; nor does he desire social disapproval as an ingrate. After Bettina parries a number of his guerrilla volleys, Nigel finally exults to find himself coincidentally alone in an abandoned cabin where Bettina is divested of her superior social and intellectual weapons and he can overcome her with brute force. Burnett establishes that Nigel's threats to rape Bettina arise less from sexual desire than from revenge for her injury to his male pride. Shortly before this scene, Nigel soliloquizes about his resentment that he does not live in an earlier era, when "women were kept in their places" (435). He visualizes hanging Bettina up and cutting her into strips, though he knows she would stare at him without uttering a sound. Later, in the cabin, Bettina lives up to his projection; though cornered and lamed from her horse having thrown her, Bettina refuses to cry, and she threatens him with the weapon Clorinda had used so effectively—Bettina promises to lash him across the mouth with her whip if he touches her. Unlike Clorinda, however, Bettina has a man to do the job for her; after overpowering Nigel in the cabin, Dunstan takes him outside, and Bettina hears Nigel howl like a dog as Dunstan whips him.

Though memorable, such sensational scenes play a relatively small role in *The Shuttle*. In addition to giving much attention to Bettina's relationship with Dunstan and her restoration of the Anstruthers estate, Burnett lightens the effect of the whole with comic scenes involving a bumptious American tourist, G. Selden, a young typewriter salesman from New York. Injuries from a bicycle accident bring him and his argot from the New York streets into the Anstruthers mansion. After overcoming his wide-eyed wonder at finding himself in the company of an American heiress and a British nobleman, Selden launches into his spiel about his typewriter and returns to New York swaggering with a letter of introduction to the Vanderpoel patriarch. Emulating Dickens, Burnett uses this commoner as a link between her more auspicious characters in New York and England as well as a complement to the capable Bettina in paying tribute to American self-confidence and ingenuity.

G. Selden provides a link to other of Burnett's works as well. He is a grown-up Little Lord Fauntleroy with the added dash of the Horatio Alger myth about the prodigious rise in fortune of American streetboys. The comic scenes in which G. Selden confronts the alien worlds of British aristocracy and American wealth were so successful that Burnett resurrected him, slightly altered, as the hero of her next romance for adults, *T. Tembarom*. In addition, Bettina's restoration of the Anstruther's estate and its lady enlarges the plot of *A Woman's Will*, as Thwaite observes;[29] and, recalling *A Little Princess*, Burnett portrays Bettina's wealth as a kind of magic that enables her to bring about these transformations. Finally, Bettina's special interest in restoring the estate gardens with the help of a proud local gardener as well as Burnett's portrayal of Bettina's nephew as a cripple forecast key features of her next romance, *The Secret Garden*, which found appreciative readers long after *The Shuttle* was forgotten.

The Secret Garden and Related Essays.   Generally recognized as Burnett's best work for children, *The Secret Garden* (1911) combines plot formulas from her earlier well-known child romances.[30] In *Little Lord Fauntleroy*, she had portrayed a child reunited with his estranged family, and in *Little Princess*, she had portrayed an orphan who finds a new family. *The Secret Garden* has both. After her parents die in India, Mary Lennox goes to live with her uncle in the Yorkshire moors; there, she befriends her hypochondriac cousin, Colin Craven, who is alienated from his embittered father; in the end, the two children and the adult form a reunited and expanded family. As in previous romances, Burnett uses motifs from the Cinderella tale. In some variants of that tale, Cinderella's dead mother aids her through a plant growing on her grave or an animal she had given to Cinderella before she died.[31] Through her portrayal of the secret garden and a robin who lives there, Burnett uses both of these motifs. Before she died giving birth to Colin, Mrs. Craven—who is also Mary Lennox's aunt—had cultivated a rose garden, where she had had a serious fall just before Colin was born. Archibald Craven blames the garden and the child for his wife's death and tries to shut both out of his life. He has the garden locked and abandoned, and he avoids the child both because Colin looks like his mother and because Craven fears the boy will inherit his own crippled back. The secret garden and the robin who inhabits it become primary agents which break the enchantment of illness and alienation which came upon the Craven family when the mother died.

The garden works first through the children. When Mary Lennox arrives in Yorkshire, she is thin and sickly, irritable and withdrawn, but the robin helps her find the key to the locked garden; and tending the garden makes her physically healthier and less self-absorbed. After her own healing is on its way, Mary discovers her cousin Colin, who is similarly spoiled and more seriously hypochondriacal; she brings Colin into the garden and he, too, becomes well. After the dead woman's garden and its robin break the enchantment over Mary and Colin, she herself calls her husband into the new circle of health. In the Austrian mountains, Craven has a dream in which he hears his dead wife call him back to the garden. There, at the end of the book, Craven finds and embraces the two healthy, happy children.

While the Cinderella tale provides an archetypal substructure for *The Secret Garden,* the first-time reader is more aware of Burnett's portrayal of her child characters and of the garden itself. In Mary Lennox, Burnett created her most complex fictional child. Complex characterization is especially difficult in children's fiction; much less than in adult fiction can the author use abstract analysis of a character's feelings and motives; internal complexities must be expressed primarily through external actions and concrete images; character change must be dramatized or symbolically suggested rather than directly described. Burnett's experience writing for the stage—learning to use dialogue and scene effectively—was put to good use in *The Se-*

cret Garden, and nowhere in her fiction were her talents as a symbolist more fully engaged. Mary Lennox's psychological change is dramatized through a succession of encounters with physical and natural objects, animals, and persons within her expanding environment. Her environment often reflects her own internal state, and her occasional recognition of this correspondence dramatizes her growth in self-awareness as she changes.

The opening chapter of *The Secret Garden* finds Mary alone and forgotten in a bungalow in India, since cholera has killed her parents and most of their servants; this physical setting underlines Mary's psychological isolation caused by being neglected by her parents and served by menials who do not love her. When discovered by an officer, Mary does not cry. In *A Little Princess,* Sara Crewe's pride had kept her from crying publicly when her father died, but Mary Lennox does not cry because she perceives no human loss; she is simply angry that her physical needs have been forgotten. A short stay with the family of an English clergyman does little to break Mary out of her protective isolation. When one of the children wants to help her make a pretend garden, Mary sends him away and earns the taunt, "Mistress Mary, quite contrary, / How does your garden grow?" (chap. 2).

Arriving at Misselthwaite, Mary initially finds no children to intrude on her private games, but a Yorkshire housemaid, Martha, inadvertantly suggests a new game by telling Mary about the locked, secret garden; Martha also lets Mary know that in England servants will not obey her every command. Searching the grounds for the secret garden, Mary meets a gardener and a robin who help her recognize her own feelings because they mirror them. Told that the robin was left alone when the rest of his brood flew away, Mary declares, "I am lonely." "She had not known before that this was one of the things which made her feel sour and cross. She seemed to find it out when the robin looked at her and she looked at the robin" (chap. 4). The gardener, Ben Weatherstaff, similarly offers a mirror for Mary. "Tha' an' me are a good bit alike," he tells her. "We're neither of us good lookin' an' we're both of us as sour as we look. We've got the same nasty tempers" (chap. 4). The secret garden offers Mary another picture of herself, for it too is a neglected orphan: "I'm the only one in the world who wants it to be alive," she says (chap. 10). By learning to respect the housemaid Martha, by befriending the robin and Ben Weatherstaff, and by taking loving charge of the secret garden,

Mary gradually gains touch with her own feelings and breaks out of her earlier isolation; this inner healing is reflected in increasing physical health and energy.

Having undergone these changes, Mary encounters the most complete picture of the child she once was in the isolated, sick, temperamental Colin. Because Colin believes he is becoming a cripple who will soon die, he stays in a remote room of the mansion where he will be seen by no one but the servants, whom he can tyrannize because they fear his tantrums may precipitate his death. In an effective example of Burnett's ability to find physical correlatives for psychological processes, she has Mary's gradual discovery of Colin symbolically suggest her own search for the unhappy self hidden inside her. Several times Mary searches the mansion for the source of a remote cry, "a curious sound—it seemed almost as if a child were crying somewhere" (chap. 5). That the children are in some senses alter egos is suggested also by their perception of each other as ghosts when they first meet. They soon break out of such solipsistic fantasies, however, for their nasty tempers make each recognize the other as a person outside his or her control.

One day when Colin calls for Mary, she works in the garden instead and that night is awakened by his screams. Angrily crying out that "Somebody ought to beat him," "savage little Mary" runs to his room and tells him, "You stop! I hate you!" Earlier in the evening, Mary had refused to let Colin manipulate her through pity, when he told her he was going to die. Now, Mary tells him, "I wish everybody would run out of the house and let you scream yourself to death!" She declares that the lump on his back is "only a hysterical lump" and demands to see it. She finds that "there's not a lump as big as a pin!" and adds, "If you ever say there is again I shall laugh!" Colin's "storm of sobbing" eventually subsides; he asks Mary, "Do you think—I could—live to grow up?" and agrees to take trips outside the house with Mary (chap. 17). No one had ever had the courage to call Colin's bluff and thus release him from his irrational fears. Mary was able to do so not only because she was angry but also because she recognized that Colin was using manipulative strategies she herself had once used.

Having dramatized the stages by which Mary breaks free from her own isolation and then springs Colin from his similar trap, Burnett portrays the completion of their psychological and physical healing primarily symbolically, through their work in the secret garden. To

explain the marvelous changes the children undergo there, Burnett
uses a metaphor from her earlier works, magic. She employs magic
to describe the power of nature to effect changes in human beings
much as it brings new life in spring after the death of winter; in
doing so, Burnett draws on a literary pastoral tradition at least as old
as Vergil's *Georgics* and allows her usual use of the fairy tale to be
transformed into myth. Like Vergil in his *Georgics* and Thoreau in
Walden, Burnett uses the seasonal cycle to give form to her work as
well as to symbolically underscore human rebirth. Mary arrives at
Misselthwaite in late winter; the two children enter the garden together in early spring; during the summer they fully recover; and in
the autumn Colin's father returns to share their harvest of health.
This emphasis on the seasonal cycle presents the children with nature
as ever changing, ever new; most often, the children marvel at the
changes spring brings continually to the garden. But the realization
that nature's cycles are themselves unchanging also brings the children occasional glimpses of what Spenser called the "eterne in muta-
bilitie."[32] At times, their hearts stand "still at the strange unchanging
majesty of the rising sun—which has been happening every morning
for thousands and thousands of years." Colin thus perceives the mystery of nature when he learns he can walk and exclaims, "I shall live
forever and ever and ever!" (chap. 20).

Also like Vergil and Thoreau, Burnett stresses the importance of
work, the human cooperation needed if nature is to achieve its best
results. By describing nature's healing power as "Magic," the children acknowledge that it is partially outside their control—the healing of themselves and their garden needs the fresh air and warmer
temperatures of spring. But the children also know that this "Magic
works best when you work yourself," as Colin puts it (chap. 26). And
so they till the garden, do physical exercises, and engage in magic
experiments to help Colin get well—they call on nature's power
through incantations and by sitting and processing in a "Mystic circle" (chap. 14). This georgic reciprocity between man and nature—
described in Wordsworth's *Prelude* as being both "willing to work and
to be wrought upon," of being "creator and receiver both"[33]—is reflected by the lyrical and incantational style of Burnett's book; language is used to celebrate what the characters receive, and it also
provides a tool with which they can work or create. After they begin
witnessing spring work its "magic" in their garden and in themselves, Mary and Colin frequently burst into lyrics of joy. Similarly,

paeans to nature rise from the lips of the Yorkshire folk the children meet, especially Ben Weatherstaff and Martha's brother, Dickon, both of whom join the children's secret garden community. Occasionally, these paeans become incantatory as well as lyrical, as when Mary soothes Colin to sleep after a tantrum with a description of spring entering the garden. Possibly incantatory as well is the children's use in the garden of the Yorkshire dialect, a language made potent by its use by the folk who have long lived intimately with nature. Language is a tool for doing also since it is a transmitter of the proverbial wisdom Hesiod and Vergil had established as part of the georgic pastoral tradition. In bringing healing to themselves and their garden, the children are aided by the lore of Ben Weatherstaff, Dickon, and especially Dickon's mother, whose proverbial wisdom is quoted often throughout the narrative.

Burnett's use of the Yorkshire folk, especially Dickon and his mother, gives mythic resonance to her work as does her use of the seasonal cycle to symbolize rebirth. Twelve-year-old Dickon is an unself-conscious nature child; first presented sitting under a tree and playing a pipe for some attending animals, he is obviously meant to suggest the nature deity Pan. Mother Sowerby, a "comfortable wonderful mother creature" (chap. 24), on the other hand, has the aura of the archetypal Earth Mother. The twelve children she has fattened on "th' air of th' moor" and "th' grass same as th' wild ponies" suggest her fertility (chap. 4). In addition, Mother Sowerby works behind the scenes on behalf of her adopted children, Mary and Colin, until she finally appears to bless their revived garden and their healthy selves. In a sense, Mother Sowerby, like the garden and its robin, is an agent for the spirit of Colin's dead mother; she is like the fairy godmother who helps Cinderella in some versions of the tale. Mother Sowerby herself points to the links in this chain of female benevolence by telling the healthy Colin, "Thy own mother's in this 'ere very garden, I do believe. She couldna' keep out of it." Adding that "Thy father mun come back to thee," Mother Sowerby sends a letter calling Craven to return, at about the same time as Craven's dead wife calls to him in a dream (chap. 27).

Burnett's portrayal of a quasi-mystical relationship between Colin's dead mother, Mother Sowerby, and the secret garden connects this juvenile classic to other works in which Burnett gave a divine aura to female power, such as *The Pretty Sister of José* and *A Lady of Quality*. *The Secret Garden* also has a significant number of parallels to Charlotte Brontë's *Jane Eyre,* as Thwaite notes.[34] Briefly, both books depict an ill-tempered orphan who lives with a family whose children taunt her and then moves to a mansion in the Yorkshire moors. Both orphans encounter secret residents who function in some ways as their doubles—Mary finds her hypochondriacal self in Colin, as has been noted, and just before her marriage to Rochester, Jane Eyre discovers his imprisoned, mad wife, a mirror image of the angry, rebellious self Jane herself has been trying to restrain. Finally, a mystical call from a distant place helps effect the happy reunion concluding each book— on the Continent, Colin's father hears his dead wife call him back to the garden much as Jane hears Rochester's call across the moors as she contemplates marriage to another.

As Sandra M. Gilbert and Susan Gubar have pointed out, *Jane Eyre* contains many of the symbolic motifs prevalent in nineteenth-century literature written by women; the relationship of *The Secret Garden* to this tradition can be seen by an analysis of Burnett's use and adaptation of these motifs. Gilbert and Gubar note the frequent depiction by female writers of "maddened doubles" or "asocial surrogates" for their protagonists, "obsessive depictions of diseases like anorexia," "metaphors" of "physical discomfort," and "images of enclosure and escape"[35]—symbolic expressions of the disintegration of the psyche, negation of the body, and psychological and physical imprisonment caused by narrow socially approved roles for women. Both Mary and her "double" Colin are sickly when they first appear, and Burnett stresses their thinness and lack of appetite. The initially dying garden provides a "metaphor" for their "physical discomfort," and its "enclosure"—the high, locked walls around it—images the physical and psychological isolation of both children when they first appear in the book. Congruent with her mode of comic romance, however, Burnett transforms these motifs of despair into images of female celebration. Through crucial adaptations of her protagonist's "double" and her "image of enclosure," Burnett allies herself with the feminist writers of the late-nineteenth century who, as Elaine Showalter has pointed out, "made the maternal instinct the basis of their ideology" and saw in this "female influence," especially over males, "a genuine source of power."[36]

Burnett exalts the maternal instinct first by making Mary's "double" a boy she can nurture; her role in Colin's recovery places Mary in the romance's chain of female power along with Colin's dead mother, Mother Sowerby, and the secret garden. Moreover, by making her "enclosure" a garden, Burnett is able to transform it from tomb to womb. It is approximately nine months from the time Mary first enters the garden, in late winter, until the children publicly exit it in the fall—happily, Burnett does not call this symbolic reinforcement to her reader's attention; it remains part of the romance's mythic substructure, of which Burnett herself was probably only partially aware. Similarly subtle but present are the suggestions of human birth in Burnett's description of the children's exit from the garden which concludes the romance. The exodus is less an "escape" than a bursting forth of an exuberant, secret life that can no longer be contained. As he approaches the garden, the returning Archibald Craven hears "the laughter of young things, the uncontrollable laughter of children who were trying not to be heard but who in a moment or so—as their excitement mounted—would burst forth." The door of the garden is suddenly "flung wide open"; and out from the walls Craven had sealed as his wife's tomb comes his healthy son Colin, "full speed" in an "unseeing dash." Following Colin is Craven's new "daughter," Mary (chap. 27). Dramatically, this final reunion is a sentimental cliché. Nevertheless, the reader who is sensitive to the symbolic resonance of its setting, the secret garden, is likely to be moved. For by now that central trope unites Burnett's chain of specifically female nurturant power with the larger mythic theme of seasonal death and rebirth in nature and in human lives, regardless of sex or age.

The Secret Garden has its flaws. Some readers might object to its sentimental idealization of poverty and the class system in its portrayal of the Sowerby family and the gardener, Ben Weatherstaff. In a brief, uncharacteristic foray into fantasy, Burnett shows events in the garden through the consciousness of the robin and his mate, and she approaches her frequent silliness when personifying animals. Near the end, Burnett mechanically and unnecessarily interprets the garden as a symbol for the human mind; this discussion of the mind's power—the danger of locking it up, the necessity of weeding out bad thoughts to plant good ones—is undoubtedly the reason some contemporary readers considered *The Secret Garden* a Christian Science book. Most readers have been willing to forgive these lapses, however, because of the romance's many layers of symbolic meaning. Clearly the best of Burnett's works for children, *The Secret Garden* is also one of the richest, most complex, and most resonant of recognized children's classics.

Two essays published as books testify to the fact that *The Secret Garden* originated in her own life experiences as well as in her former child romances and her reading of works by others. In response to a letter asking about the "original" of the robin in *The Secret Garden*, Burnett wrote *My Robin* (1912), a sentimental description of a bird she befriended during writing sessions in her garden at Maytham, in Kent. Far more convincing and moving is *In the Garden*, written while Burnett was propped up in bed during her final illness, and published posthumously in 1925. As Burnett's activities outside her home had decreased, Burnett had given free reign to her lifelong love of gardening. In the tradition of Vergil's encomium on farming in his *Georgics*, Burnett now passed on her lore through detailed descriptions of gardens and gardening in every season; also, as Vergil had exhorted his readers to farm, Burnett declared that "every one in the world really wants a garden" and "can have one," "if it is only two yards wide."[37] The rewards are those Burnett had described in *The Secret Garden:* "As long as one has a garden one has a future; and as long as one has a future one is alive" (10, 30). This and other sentences in the essay have a significance probably not intended by an author who, initially at least, did not expect that it would be primarily her writing for children that would live on after her. Burnett wrote better, perhaps, than she knew when she observed, "There are a number of things and conditions which will provide futures, . . . but no one of them seems so natural, so simple and so alluring as making a garden" (11).

T. Tembarom.   Burnett followed her juvenile masterpiece, *The Secret Garden,* with what many readers might consider the best of her long romances for adults. Serialized in the *Century* and published as a book in 1913, *T. Tembarom* shows Burnett forty-five years into her publishing career still able to find fresh entertainment possibilities in character types and formulas she had used often before; the chief prototypes for *T. Tembarom* also demonstrate the intimate relationship between her romances for children and for adults. The immediate impulse for *T. Tembarom* was to capitalize on the popularity of the American typewriter salesman, G. Selden, in *The Shuttle*. Like G. Selden, the title character of *T. Tembarom* has learned to survive in the New York City commercial world without benefit of family connections; and in both romances Burnett delights in parading her young American, with his frank manner and colorful slang, before the British aristocracy.

The circumstances under which T. Tembarom finds himself in England, however, show that the romance in which he figures is ultimately a revision for adults of Burnett's first best-seller for children, *Little Lord Fauntleroy*. In the opening chapters of *T. Tembarom*, a British lawyer arrives to tell the young newspaper reporter that he is heir to the Temple Barholm estate in northern England—"T. Tembarom" had been a "school-boy modification" of "Temple Temple Barholm," considered "absurd and pretentious" for a boy orphaned at ten who ran errands and sold newspapers to support himself (chap. 1). And so, like Cedric Errol in *Little Lord Fauntleroy*, T. Tembarom suddenly finds himself having virtually unlimited money and being treated like a lord; also like Cedric, T. Tembarom must demonstrate that his goodness and nobility are innate; he must prove incorruptible by money and social prestige and face their probable loss with equanimity when a rival heir appears.

In writing *T. Tembarom*, Burnett borrowed from *Little Lord Fauntleroy* not only its general plot outline but also much of the personality of its main character; and she obviously enjoyed the game of finding out what her most famous fictional character would be like grown up—in one scene, T. Tembarom looks at a painting of one of his ancestors and asks "Who's this Fauntleroy in the lace collar?" (chap. 13) Like his fictional ancestor, T. Tembarom is empathetic, eager to please, free of personal vanity, unready to take offense, and seemingly unconscious of his winsome way with people. Naturally democratic, he enjoys without condescension the company of servants and cottagers; naturally noble, he uses his fortune to correct injustices the world has dealt to others.

T. Tembarom's two most important crusades begin even before he steps on the boat for England. In his New York rooming house, he has befriended a Lancashire commoner, Mr. Hutchinson, who has been trying unsuccessfully to sell a railroad invention. T. Tembarom has also fallen in love with Mr. Hutchinson's daughter, "Little Ann," an "early Victorian" "apotheosis of the feminine," who strikes men as both babylike and motherly (chaps. 15, 2). Curiously asexual, as is the essentially childlike T. Tembarom, Little Ann nevertheless continues the exaltation of feminine nurturant power shown in *The Secret Garden*. Without letting him suspect it, Ann skillfully manages her father's business as well as domestic affairs; and it is she, not T. Tembarom, who directs their course of love. She refuses his marriage proposal after he learns of his new fortune and title; before he commits himself to someone who drops her *h*'s (chap. 8), Ann says, T. Tembarom must see what aristocratic life is like and make himself vulnerable to the charms of young ladies featured in British illustrated weeklies. Being both obedient child and medieval knight, as Little Lord Fauntleroy had been, T. Tembarom accepts his lady love's charge, and he spends his last days in New York introducing Hutchinson's invention to influential businessmen his new fortune and fame now allow him to meet.

T. Tembarom's second major crusade begins when, still a newspaper reporter, he brings home an amnesiac he had found wandering the New York streets. Dubbing the amnesiac "Strangeways," T. Tembarom takes him to England, and in the most amazing of coincidences Burnett allows herself in this fairy tale for adults, Strangeways turns out to be Jem Barholm, the real Temple Barholm heir, who had been thought killed during a building cave-in in the Klondike. The combination of T. Tembarom's crusades on behalf of Mr. Hutchinson and Jem Barholm provides the happy ending to Burnett's romance. By the time Barholm has recovered his memory and is ready to assume his inheritance, Mr. Hutchinson's invention has gained him great wealth and a British title, so that when T. Tembarom marries Ann, he can share the money he had helped earn.

In addition to demonstrating how Burnett frequently used the same character types and plot formulas in writing for children and adults, *T. Tembarom,* like the earlier *A Little Princess,* shows how her romances often benefitted from her knowledge of the stage. As usual, Burnett has her main character compare his experiences to events typical in fiction—in a fairy tale, in a medieval romance, in a three-volume, sentimental novel (chaps. 2, 8–9, 26, 29). In addition, there are an unusual number of comparisons to the theater. The sudden inheritance of a vast fortune strikes T. Tembarom as "a turn at a vaudeville" or a "farce" (chaps. 6–7) for example; and the romance's climactic scenes, which resolve the inheritance controversy, are compared to the fourth act of a melodrama (chaps. 32, 38). However, despite some touches of melodrama, which Burnett almost always included in her fairy tales for children and adults, the dominant tone of *T. Tembarom* is comic. Vivian Burnett accurately described the romance as having "the makings of an exceptional 'comedy of manners,' "[38] and Burnett spent considerable time during her later years working on a dramatic version which was apparently never finished or produced. As it stands, *T. Tembarom* represents Burnett's longest and most sustained excursion into social comedy.

T. Tembarom, like *Little Lord Fauntleroy*, takes a lighthearted look at some differences between American and British societies. By the time she wrote the adult romance, however, Burnett had had twenty-eight more years of observing and writing about life on both sides of the Atlantic and was able to portray these differences in greater detail. Also, since her protagonist is twenty-five rather than seven when he goes to England, he can be used to display a wider range of American values and manners. As in *Little Lord Fauntleroy*, Burnett has fun with her protagonist's reactions to his new life in Britain; in addition, however, some of the adult romance's cleverest humor stems from the impression her "common American lad" (chap. 6) makes on various British "types" who see him through the filter of preconceptions, usually unflattering, they have of Americans. T. Tembarom fits their preconceptions in enough ways so that, at least initially, the British are puzzled about his true nature. Some consistently underrate him while others recognize his genuine intelligence and good nature despite his strange values and ways. As in some of Burnett's other romances, notably *A Little Princess* and *Little Lord Fauntleroy*, *T. Tembarom* stresses the importance of being able to read character correctly, despite deceptive appearances.

Chief among the British types who are soon charmed by T. Tembarom's American manner and good nature are—in addition to the Hutchinsons—T. Tembarom's valet, a poor relation, and an eccentric lord. T. Tembarom's first encounters with his valet are among the most successful comic scenes in the romance. With their clever dialogue, description of gesture, and indication of various kind of "business," these scenes beg for presentation on the stage. Master and servant are equally eager to please but unsure of what is expected of them. T. Tembarom knows nothing of the "fearsome" "ceremony of dressing," feels like a "fool," and knows that "there is no way out of looking like one." Pearson, the valet, has heard from the other servants that his new master is "likely to be American enough to swagger and bluster and pretend he knew everything better than any one else, and lose his temper frightfully when he made mistakes, and try to make other people seem to blame." Pearson is thus afraid he will lose his job if, for example, he tells his master that he has nothing suitable to wear at dinner; but the valet also fears he will lose his own "well-earned reputation" if he allows his master to appear in public inappropriately dressed (chap. 11). After a good deal of maladroit maneuvering during which each unsuccessfully tries to anticipate the movements of the other, T. Tembarom takes a direct approach. "You're not half as rattled as I am," T. Tembarom confesses. Pearson's dancing around him gives him "the Willies," and he is resolved that "little Willie is going to put on his own socks" (chap. 12). He will double Pearson's wages *not* to valet him; instead, Pearson will serve T. Tembarom's charge, the anmnesiac. When T. Tembarom makes plans to bring from London Pearson's fiancée, a lady's maid, Pearson's loyalty to his new master is assured.

Similarly won over are Miss Alicia Barholm and Lord Stone. Like Little Ann Hutchinson, the penniless spinster, Miss Alicia, is described as an "astonishingly perfect" "early-Victorian" "type" (chap. 14)—a nostalgia for the Victorian era surfaced increasingly in Burnett's fiction as the twentieth century progressed. Finding himself exceedingly lonely in the Temple Barholm "museum" (chap. 12) and desiring to create for himself a "little *family*" (chap. 29), T. Tembarom makes Miss Alicia matron of his house and the eccentric Lord Stone his fatherly confidant.

Notable among the British types baffled by this "common American lad" are the estate lawyer, a self-aggrandizing society matron and her haughty daughter, and a gentleman schemer. At times, they believe that T. Tembarom's generosity and ignorance of British manners make him a ready tool for their own schemes; at other times, they suspect that his open, good nature is only a facade to hide some scheme of his own. The suspicion and scheming of these Britains add touches of melodrama to Burnett's romance as well as give bite to its frequent humor at the Britains' expense. The lawyer, Palford, who finds T. Tembarom in New York and escorts him to England, is the first to suspect that T. Tembarom may be more than he seems. Initially, he finds this "cheap young man in cheap clothes, and speaking New York slang with a nasal accent" "a positive encyclopedia of lack of knowledge" about not only British history and customs but his own national past. At times, however, Palford wonders if T. Tembarom is not making him the butt of American dead-pan humor. While Palford shows the new heir the Temple Barholm mansion, for example, Palford notes that T. Tembarom sometimes makes "a totally absurdly exaggerated or seemingly ignorance-revealing observation" "with an unmoved expression of gravity" which leaves the "hearer to decide for himself whether the speaker . . . [is] an absolute ignoramus and fool or a humorist." And Palford wonders if T. Tembarom is trying " 'to get a rise out of him,' after the odious manner of the tourists described in [Mark Twain's] 'Innocent's Abroad' " (chaps. 7, 13).

Palford is correct, of course, in suspecting that the new Temple Barholm heir is more formidable than he appears; his good nature is genuine, but it does not make him a fool. T. Tembarom proves more than equal, for example, to Lady Joan, one of the last in Burnett's considerable line of female spitfires. Because they are penniless, Lady Joan's mother urges her to win T. Tembarom as a husband. Lady Joan will have none of him, however, not only because she regards him as uncouth but also because she had been in love with Jem Barholm and resents this American upstart who has taken Jem's place. Burnett's handling of T. Tembarom's confrontations with Lady Joan is typical of the victories she gives her American lad over the British who try to set themselves up as his adversaries: T. Tembarom simultaneously shames them with his good nature and proves that he can beat them at their own game. The grace with which T. Tembarom suffers Lady Joan's insults proves that though educated in the New York streets he is more noble than she. When Lady Joan mistakenly assumes T. Tembarom plans to marry her and derides him for his presumption, he ingenuously tells her that his heart already belongs to another and that in observing Lady Joan's undeniable charms, he had only been following his true love's bidding. T. Tembarom convinces Lady Joan that he sympathizes with her for the loss of her true love, however, and she remains loyal to him when mistaken interpretations of T. Tembarom's character become libelous in the climactic scenes of the book.

The perpetrator of this libel is the scheming gentleman, Palliser—the name was no doubt borrowed from the society novels of Anthony Trollope. The encounters between Palliser and T. Tembarom are the romance's best examples of Burnett's skill in using national character types to create dramatic conflict as well as humor. Palliser takes one step further the estate lawyer's suspicion that T. Tembarom is an American dead-pan humorist trying to make a fool of his listener. Palliser concludes that T. Tembarom is a "Yankee trickster" who uses a facade of "candor and almost primitive good nature" to throw others "off guard" while he lines his own pockets. Assuming that T. Tembarom's nature is as mercenary as his own, Palliser tries to convince the American to join a questionable investment scheme to which he himself is overcommitted—in another playful reference to *Little Lord Fauntleroy,* Burnett calls the investment firm "the Cedric." Confident of his knowledge of the type he is dealing with—"I know New York though I have n't lived there"—Palliser appeals to T. Tembarom's supposed pride in his "sharp" "American method" of negotiating business: "Your air of ingenuous ignorance is the cleverest thing about you," he tells T. Tembarom (chaps. 19, 33).

Palliser fails in this investment scheme, however, because T. Tembarom also proves a student of national types and recognizes the British gentleman's way of throwing an opponent "off guard." "The very way his clothes fit, the style he's got his hair brushed, that swell, careless lounge of his" are calculated, T. Tembarom says, to make it seem that Palliser is simply "a gentleman visiting round among his friends and a million miles from wanting to butt in with business." Though T. Tembarom is not taken in by Palliser's performances, he does admire "the top notch way he does it." Proving that he is indeed an American dead-pan humorist, if not the Yankee trickster Palliser believes him, T. Tembarom makes a fool of Palliser by pretending an interest in the investment scheme just to watch the British gentleman embroider his act. Palliser "gets in such fine work that I switch him on to it whenever I want cheering up," T. Tembarom tells his confidant, Lord Stone; "it makes me sorter forget things that worry me" (chap. 28).

When Palliser's flattery and appeals to T. Tembarom's pocket book fail, he turns to blackmail. Having gained a surreptitious look at T. Tembarom's closeted amnesiac, Palliser had recognized him as Jem Barholm. He accuses T. Tembarom of guarding his inheritance by isolating Jem so that he can spirit him away to a remote insane asylum should this rightful heir regain his memory. When Palliser threatens to expose this nefarious scheme, T. Tembarom "jollies" him "along" in his assumptions (chap. 19), hoping he can soon prove Palliser wrong. He has been keeping Barholm isolated because of his fragile mental state; meanwhile, he has quietly consulted a London nerve specialist and sought more information to verify the amnesiac's identity. When both T. Tembarom and the amnesiac mysteriously disappear from the estate, Palliser reveals his suspicions to the world. The romance's climactic scenes are aptly compared, by T. Tembarom, to the fourth act of a melodrama. All external circumstances support Palliser's inference that T. Tembarom is a villain. And Burnett skillfully manages to get most of her considerable cast of characters on-stage to hear Palliser make his accusations and to witness T. Tembarom's presentation of the recovered Jem Barholm as the true heir. Lord Stone, who has long been privy to T. Tembarom's secret plans, verifies the consistent nobility of the young American's motives. And T. Tembarom declares that the gathered company has just witnessed a melodrama without a villain—Burnett suggests that Palliser was more the "fool" of her good-natured young American humorist than a genuine villain (chap. 39).

T. Tembarom is the last of Burnett's romances about Americans in Britain—she has no British protagonists come to America. Having a dual British-American identity herself and a reading public on both sides of the Atlantic, Burnett always tried to show neither society to disadvantage in her fictional comparisons. In *Little Lord Fauntleroy* and *The Shuttle,* she dramatized the benefits of combining the best of both through intermarriage. Cedric Errol is an ideal child not least because he has an American mother as well as a British father, and the marriage of Bettina Vanderpoel and Lord Dunstan is intended to symbolize the ideal cooperation between the American frontier spirit and British respect for history and tradition. Since by the last pages it is assumed that the Americans will spend most of the rest of their lives enjoying their British titles and estates, however, these romances can be said to tilt toward Britain.

A Fair Barbarian and *T. Tembarom,* on the other hand, give America the rose, though neither is intended to offend a British reader. In *A Fair Barbarian,* it will be recalled, a young American woman wins the admiration of a provincial British town and turns down its prize bachelor to marry her American lover. T. Tembarom similarly wins the affections of most Britains and outwits those who oppose him. His bride, Ann Hutchinson, is from Lancashire, but they set up housekeeping in New York City, the bustle of which T. Tembarom sorely missed during his stay in England. In her final chapter, Burnett describes how the American press delights in the Horatio Alger myth T. Tembarom personifies. " 'In spite of all temptations to belong to other nations,' he had been born in Brooklyn," "had worn ragged clothes," and had "sold newspapers there." Moreover, Burnett's description of the newlyweds' domestic arrangements is a smiling paean to the American frontier spirit and bourgeois values. They have chosen a "very new" apartment house in a neighborhood that is just being settled and still has a "frankly unfinished air" about it.

Everything is "exceedingly fresh and clean," including the lavishly
ornamented apartment building with its attention to creature com-
forts. In the final scene, T. Tembarom, laden with purchases, comes
home to Ann unpacking and making things tidy. As night falls, they
watch the lights of the New York City skyline and feel they are living in a "dream" (chap. 40). Though Burnett does not specifically say
so, it is a quintessentially American dream.

T. Tembarom deserves a prominent place in Burnett's oeuvre not
only because of its contribution to the British-American theme in her
fiction but also because of its quality. The cleverness and complexity
of its social comedy are unexcelled in Burnett's fiction, though as in
her other long popular romances for adults, she was not able to extend the excitement of her good scenes through her entire narrative.
Since T. Tembarom does not take its melodrama so seriously, however,
it has greater tonal unity then In Connection with The De Willoughby
Claim or The Shuttle; and it engages in less self-indulgent repetition
than either of these works or the vastly inferior romances she published two years before she died. As expressions of Burnett's humor,
some readers may prefer the shorter, less ambitious, but more fully
realized Making of a Marchioness. Of Burnett's long romances for
adults, however, T. Tembarom remains the most entertaining.

The Lost Prince and the Last Adult Romances.   In 1914, the
year after she published T. Tembarom, Burnett returned to America
from what would be her last trip to Europe and spent the rest of her
life on her estates on Long Island and Bermuda; in her fiction, however, she looked back across the Atlantic. The Lost Prince (1915), for
children, and the linked adult romances, The Head of the House of
Coombe and Robin, both published in 1922, reflected Burnett's concern about the effect of world war on the European countries she had
come to love. Burnett saw the war as bringing to an end the era of
Western civilization to which she belonged; while she tried to maintain the optimism about the future characteristic of her fiction, all
three of her last romances express a strong nostalgia for the past.

The Lost Prince pays tribute to royal privilege and pageantry, which
World War I caused to "crash in ruins," as Burnett later put it in
"The Passing the Kings" (1919), an elegiac account of royalty she
had observed during her lifetime. Explaining that her infatuation
with royalty began when she "was a child, because their ways and
belongings were the only things that were like fairy stories," Burnett
describes the royal pageantry she observed during her last trip

through Europe in 1913 and 1914, "just on the eve of the passing of emperors and kings from the face of the earth." She had seen so many of "those royal persons who today are fleeing and . . . trembling in castles while their people rave and howl in their capitals' streets."[39] This trip provided the specific as well as general imaginative impulse for *The Lost Prince*. In Vienna, she had been struck by the resemblance of a Van Dyke portrait of a Bavarian prince to her dead son Lionel, and her resulting musings contributed to the main character in *The Lost Prince*.[40] Also, the Archduke Ferdinand of Austria was assassinated in Sarajevo just the month before she returned to the United States, and the role of Serbian nationalism in precipitating world war is reflected in Burnett's portrayal of her fictional Samavia. Small, mountainous, once-Edenic Samavia is in political chaos and leaders in various European capitals fear the turmoil may spread; some are allies of a secret Samavian society to bring from exile the descendant of a prince lost during a civil war five hundred years before.

While *The Lost Prince* was precipitated by twentieth-century events and changes, its story reads much "like a legend from the Middle Ages," as Burnett observes near its end (chap. 30). It focuses on the journey throughout Europe of the lost prince's twelve-year-old son and his street urchin friend to alert political sympathizers of the prince's imminent return to Samavia; and the book closes with that prince's accession to the throne and restoration of Samavian peace. Burnett's romance thus combines two mythic motifs, the perilous journey and the return of the king; and it combines these motifs much as would J. R. R. Tolkien's fantasy trilogy, *The Lord of the Rings* (1954–56). While the adults make a military assault on their enemies in Samavia—much as the exiled king Aragorn leads his troops against the wicked wizard Sauron—the two children make a journey successful largely because they are too small and apparently insignificant to be observed—much as Tolkien's hobbits journey quietly into Sauron's stronghold.

In characterizing her child heroes, Burnett, like Tolkien in his two hobbits, follows the tradition of Cervantes's Don Quixote and Sancho Panza. The lost prince's son, Marco, is idealistic and serious, while his street urchin friend, "Rat," is almost cynical and often provides comic relief. Like the male heirs who preceded him, Marco has been given an education appropriate to a royal line hoping to return; he has learned historical and geographical details of Samavia and the various European cities in which he, his father, and their servant have lived—Marco's mother is dead, and, uncharacteristic for Burnett, the book contains only a few, peripheral female characters. Aware only that his father is part of a secret society for restoring the lost prince to Samavia, Marco is unaware of his father's identity until he sees his father crowned at the end of the book. Here, as elsewhere in her fiction—in *Little Lord Fauntleroy* and *A Little Princess,* for example— Burnett uses the method described by Aristotle for heightening the effect of a dramatic climax; she has recognition of her main character's identity coincide with his radical change in fortune. To do so in this book, however, Burnett allows her hero to seem slow-witted, since evidence for the identity of Marco's father as the lost prince is so apparent earlier.

Marco's street urchin friend, who with the reader deduces the truth long before Marco does, is in many ways more interesting as a character. Making the long trek across Europe using a crutch, Rat is one of the significant number of male cripples Burnett included in her fiction during this period, as Thwaite observes—the others are Bettina's nephew in *The Shuttle;* the "self-induced cripple," Colin Craven, and his hunchbacked father in *The Secret Garden;* a poor boy befriended by T. Tembarom; and the title character in *The Little Hunchback Zia.* Thwaite conjectures that this motif was prompted by Burnett's memory of Swan Burnett's lame leg and her "continued interest in the Invalid Children's Aid Association," in addition to its being "a recipe for instant pathos."[41] The element of pathos in Rat's character is overshadowed, however, by his strong will and fertile imagination; in his love for imaginative games, Rat is a literary descendant of Mark Twain's Tom Sawyer. Rat has been infatuated with the legend of the Samavian lost prince before Marco first meets him drilling a squad of street boys in London; Marco joins their military games, and Rat devises an imaginary plan for the two to carry a secret sign to Samavian sympathizers. Much as Tom Sawyer's imaginary outlaws lead him to meeting a real outlaw in Injun Joe, Rat's game plan becomes real when the boys make their journey across Europe. In adopting Rat's plan as part of his military strategy, Marco's father observes, "Perhaps only boyhood . . . could have dared imagine it" (chap. 18).

Probably a more direct influence on *The Lost Prince,* however, was Rudyard Kipling's *Kim* (1901). Kipling's book had portrayed a young prince traveling in disguise and playing "The Great Game" of spying in India. Kim had encountered Oriental mysticism by becoming the student of a Lama, and Burnett uses an encounter Marco's father, Loristan, has with a Himalayan Buddhist to introduce again in her fiction her theosophical speculations. From the Buddhist, Loristan learns that since the human mind is part of "the Big Thought" that created the world (chap. 21), it can learn to tap that Big Thought's power. When he becomes king, Loristan plans to teach his subjects that power's laws of light, order, love, and peace. He has already made an initiate of his son Marco, who instructs Rat in this combination of religion and control of mind over body. Marco's ability to tap the power of his own mind and of the "Big Thought" help him several times in his journey; imprisoned in a dark cellar by his enemies, for example, Marco uses mind control to remain calm while he devises methods of escape; later, the operation of the "Big Thought's" power on Marco's behalf explains a coincidence through which Marco finds one of the intended receivers of his message.

The amount of attention given Burnett's theosophical concerns may explain why *The Lost Prince,* despite its scenes of engaging adventure and mythic plot, has not found as many appreciative readers as *Little Lord Fauntleroy, A Little Princess,* or *The Secret Garden.* There are other probable reasons as well, however, such as flaws in craftsmanship, for example, Marco's incredibly slow recognition of his father's and his own identity, and unnecessary repetition. In addition, many readers may be unsympathetic to Burnett's adulation of royalty and aristocracy, expressed more emphatically in *The Lost Prince* than in earlier books. A great deal is made of Loristan's kingly presence, which impresses many besides his Samavian followers; the exaggerated obeisance of his servant, Lazarus, is not tempered by the acerbic temper and wry humor that made more palatable Ben Weatherstaff's service to his master in *The Secret Garden;* Rat's cleverness and heroism are in large part explained by his father's having been a gentleman; and even among some Pekingese spaniels the boys see, one, though small, shows himself to be "the master" (chap. 19).

Burnett underscores such suggestions of the natural privilege of the royal and the aristocratic by giving a religious aura to Samavian nationalism. The prince who had left Samavia five hundred years before had been strong and handsome as "a young Viking god" (chap. 3). His descendants, Loristan and Marco, elicit from their followers not only obedience but also worship. Entering Samavia to make the last delivery of their message, Marco and Rat find "The Forgers of the Sword," who meet secretly in a cave featuring a stone "altar" with a portrait of the legendary prince hanging above it; led by a priest, the men kneel to Marco and kiss his feet in what appears to Rat a "religious ceremony" (chap. 27). After Marco has become the crown prince, Burnett describes the "strange and superstitious worship" the Samavians have for the boy "because he seemed so surely their Lost Prince restored in body and soul . . . some of them half believed when he stood in the sunshine, with the halo about his head" (chap. 31).

Burnett's adulation of royalty and the aristocracy, and even the religious aura she gives Samavian nationalism might seem appropriate if *The Lost Prince* were indeed "a legend from the Middle Ages." But because of its setting in the nineteenth century (an opera by Wagner is being performed at the Munich opera), its echo of the Balkan crises which opened the first twentieth-century world war, and its anticipation of the atavistic, quasi-religious nationalism which culminated in the second twentieth-century world war, Burnett's fictional tribute to royalism may make some readers uncomfortable. Though often engaging when read simply as an adventure romance and a tribute to boyhood heroism, *The Lost Prince* now seems a curious mixture of theosophical speculation, nostalgia for the Middle Ages and nineteenth century, and commentary on early twentieth-century nationalism.

Artistically inferior to almost anything Burnett had published since her earliest potboilers for ladies' magazine fiction, *The Head of the House of Coombe* and *Robin* are of interest primarily as indications of Burnett's response to World War I and certain changes in twentieth-century life. Originally serialized as one book in *Good Housekeeping* beginning in 1921, *The Head of the House of Coombe* was expanded and published as two books with separate titles in 1922. Set entirely in Britain during the early decades of the twentieth century, the two books are linked, in the foreground, by a highly romantic and melodramatic love story and, in the background, by the anticipation and reality of World War I.

While *The Lost Prince* expressed Burnett's nostalgia for the monarchical power and pageantry that diminished during the war, *The Head of the House of Coombe* and *Robin* pay tribute to the values, especially the aristocratic values, of the prewar era. In "The Passing of the Kings" she observed, "it may be rather witty to refer to days or morals or manners as Early Victorian. But when all is said and done, . . . Victorian days seem decently well-behaved ones, and untheatrical, and honest—and kind" (119). It is thus not surprising that in her last romances Burnett made most of her commentary on the war and social change through conversations between two characters who as aristocratic survivors from the Victorian era shared a point of view much like her own. The dowager duchess of Darte and the aging, dashing, and politically astute Lord Coombe make comments about Germany and its kaiser which perhaps amend Burnett's sympathetic portrayal of quasi-religious nationalism in *The Lost Prince*. Alternately describing the kaiser as "a mad dog loose among us" and a "terrific military bogeyman," Darte and Coombe score him for teaching in all German churches and schools the "Faith" that God is the kaiser's own "modest henchman" and that the world exists only to be "conquered and ravaged" by his war machine.[42] In addition, Burnett suggests that the war precipitated by the excesses of German nationalism will drastically alter the aristocratic social structures she nostalgically portrayed in *The Lost Prince*. Noting that the kaiser aims to achieve what Napoleon only dreamed, Darte and Coombe fear that the coming "World Revolution" will be another "French Revolution" with its "Reign of Terror" (*C,* 210, 202, 206). As the war begins to unfold, Burnett describes it as "the Second Deluge . . . carrying upon its flood old civilizations broken from anchor and half submerged as they tossed on the rising and raging waves."[43] Darte, Coombe, and their author recognize the inevitability of this war and its attendant social changes, but they hope that some of the best values from the "old civilization" they represent will survive in the younger generation who will help to rebuild the world when the war is over.

Darte and Coombe work toward this goal by becoming surrogate parents to fatherless Robin and Donal, whose love story provides the foreground plot uniting *The Head of the House of Coombe* and *Robin*. Donal is the legal heir of bachelor Lord Coombe, and early in the first romance Coombe assumes financial responsibility for Robin and her widowed mother. Robin and Donal fall in love as children but are abruptly separated. As an adolescent, Robin becomes Duchess Darte's companion and personal charge, and at the conclusion of *The Head of the House of Coombe* the young couple are reunited at a ball on the day the Archduke Ferdinand is shot. *Robin* begins with the couple's secret romance and marriage before Donal goes to fight on the Continent. Word arrives that he has been killed, Robin learns that she is pregnant but cannot prove she had been married, and Lord Coombe marries her to save her respectability and give her child his name. This noble gesture proves unnecessary, however, for after Robin bears a

son, Donal surprisingly returns from a German prison camp, and
their reunion provides the conclusion to the second romance.

As recipients of the guidance of the wise Victorians, Duchess Darte
and Lord Coombe, and as heirs of "the house of Coombe," Robin,
Donal, and their son are intended to symbolize hope for some continuity of social, particularly aristocratic, values after the war is over.
Burnett also uses the couple to symbolize her faith that late nineteenth-century explorations of the mind's frontiers and human evolution generally would continue. After word arrives that Donal is
dead, pregnant Robin is dying from her grief until Donal begins to
appear regularly in her dreams, letting her know that he wants her
and their child to live. When he returns, Donal explains that another
prisoner, an American conversant in "New Thought and Theosophy
and Christian Science" (R, 340), had taught him to send his soul to
Robin while he dreamed. Burnett goes to some length to establish
the credibility of these dream visitations, and she says that the
trauma of war has increased the number of persons having such experiences. Thus, while Burnett details and bemoans the human cost
of war, she also says that it brings out the best in people and suggests
that such cataclysms often impel a leap in human evolution (R, 35).
Recalling Bergson's concept of elán vital, Burnett speaks of God as
the "Creative Intention" and the "Great Impeller" (C, 103, 360). It
is this "force" which brings Robin and Donal together, allows a
mystical union of their souls when they are separated, and motivates
them to survive and thus help "the Creative Cause" move toward its
"intention" of "human perfection" (C, 107).

If Robin and Donal symbolize Burnett's hopes for the future, Robin's mother, "Feather," represents much that Burnett found
distasteful in modern life. The most provocative character in the two
romances, Feather can be read as Burnett's commentary on the early
twentieth-century version of the "new woman," the flapper. Feather
is empty-headed and anti-intellectual; is interested primarily in her
scanty, fashionable clothes; and has at least the aura of being sexually
promiscuous. She is also financially irresponsible and accepts an un-
respectable dependence on a man—society understandably but erro-
neously assumes she is Coombe's mistress; Coombe offers his help
both because Feather physically resembles a love of his youth and because he sees Feather is so unable to manage her life that without his
help she would be passed from one man to another. In addition,

Feather commits the cardinal sin in Burnett's decalogue for women of being a bad mother. Indeed, she is no mother at all, for motherhood mars her image of herself as a young girl. When Robin is a young child, Feather cares only that governesses dress her prettily for occasional social appearances. Later, Feather resents Robin's adolescent bloom and gladly gives her to Duchess Darte's charge. To underscore Feather's sins, Burnett resurrects the character "Dearest" from *Little Lord Fauntleroy:* She gives Donal a mother who devotes herself entirely to her child. Maintaining her nineteenth-century view of the "new woman," which included a measure of independence from men and an emphasis on female nurturing, Burnett scores the flapper for rejecting both of these responsibilities.

Burnett's portrayal of Feather is of biographical interest as well, as Thwaite points out. Feather's name recalls Burnett's own nickname, "Fluffy," and Feather's character is "a caricature . . . of all the tendencies in [Burnett] herself that frightened her, of things she had been accused of by the newspapers"—being "pleasure-loving, frivolous, extravagant"; having "no taste or feeling"; and selfishly parading her children publicly in fancy clothes.[44] It should be added that Feather's name also recalls the "light" side of Bertha Amory's personality, in *Through One Administration*—the light side Burnett herself pursued when she decided to develop herself as a popular entertainer rather than a "serious" aspirant to "the world of actual literature."[45] Read thus, Burnett's portrayal of Feather in the last of her popular romances has the marks of a pathetic, if probably unconscious, exorcism; Burnett not only embroiders Feather's sins unmercifully but also has her obliterated in a bombing raid—searchers find only her ringed hand clutching a purple scarf (*R,* 312).

Unfortunately, *The Head of the House of Coombe* and *Robin* also show Burnett at her worst as a popular romance writer. They are sentimental, melodramatic, and grossly overwritten. Burnett tries to wring too many tears from her reader in response to Robin's motherless childhood. She describes in absurd detail how her six- and eight-year-old Robin and Donal fall in love in an Edenic garden and then suffer the throes of lovesickness when they are separated. Lord Coombe makes a last-minute rescue of adolescent Robin from the clutches of a German spy who had abducted her to seduce her. And Burnett's repetitive praise of beautiful, virtuous Robin and "young superman" (*R,* 77) Donal recalls the excessive paeans given the noble couple in

His Grace of Osmonde, published twenty-five years before. Though the romances sold well, they were justifiably panned by the critics as "the apotheosis of Burnettian slush." One critic noted that "this is a pity, because once upon a time Mrs. Burnett could write differently";[46] published just two years before her death, however, these last romances undoubtedly accelerated the twentieth-century decline in her critical reputation.

Chapter Five

The Achievement of Frances Hodgson Burnett

Frances Hodgson Burnett's reputation as a superior children's author remains secure. Largely because they capture the timeless wonder of the fairy tale, Burnett's best children's books—*Little Lord Fauntleroy, A Little Princess,* and *The Secret Garden*—can entertain a child and often an adult reader almost a century after they were written, an unusual longevity for children's fiction. In addition, *The Secret Garden* joins the rank of children's classics able to reward the kind of interpretation and analysis ordinarily given to adult literature; this achievement is especially notable because so many others in this category—such as *Alice in Wonderland,* some of George MacDonald's literary fairy tales, *Wind in the Willows, The Hobbit*—belong to the genre of fantasy, which at least in children's fiction more easily yields the kind of symbolic complexity and mythic resonance found in *The Secret Garden.* Even a critic trying to resurrect some of Burnett's adult fiction from its near oblivion will probably admit that the survival of *The Secret Garden* as Burnett's masterpiece is just.

In addition to these three best and best-known books for children, Burnett made other significant contributions to the literature of childhood during the late nineteenth and early twentieth centuries. As the portrait of the artist as a child and an exploration of a child's mind and how it is often misunderstood by adults, Burnett's memoir, *The One I Knew the Best of All,* stands up well beside the better-known *Golden Age* and *Dream Days* by Kenneth Grahame. *In the Closed Room* effectively captures a ghostly aura as it confronts childhood innocence with death. Though artistically flawed and dated by Burnett's theosophical speculations and nostalgia for a royalist and aristocratic past, *The Lost Prince* nevertheless demonstrates considerable facility in the child's adventure romance. And finally, through her stage adaptations of *Little Lord Fauntleroy, Sara Crewe,* and *Racketty-Packetty House,* Burnett made notable contributions to children's theater.

Burnett's significance as a children's author lies not simply in the longevity of a few of her books and the considerable quality of others less known. A survey of her career also tells much about the nature and development of children's literature, particularly in its relationship to adult literature, the education of children, and popular culture. Through their idealization of the innocence and imagination of the child, their use of the fairy tale and pastoral themes, Burnett's books for children and her childhood memoir join children's classics such as those by Lewis Carroll, Mark Twain, George MacDonald, and Kenneth Grahame to show how much of the first golden age of children's literature owed to the earlier Romantic movement in adult literature. Also, Burnett's books demonstrate the continuity of many nineteenth-century children's classics with the earlier tradition of children's literature, closely tied to the schoolbook. In her child romances, Burnett conflated the magical transformation typical of the fairy tale with the conversion of others, often adults, brought about by the model child in the moral and religious exemplum. The same didactic tradition can be seen in Louisa May Alcott's *Little Women,* which presents a series of the girls' moral adventures, with their mother providing the didactic commentary. Even Mark Twain paid the exemplum the compliment of inverting it; in Tom Sawyer and Huck Finn, he elevated the Sunday School picture of the "bad" boy into a new ideal and satirized the "good" boy in Tom's tattletale brother Sid and the "model boy," Willie Mufferson.

Finally, Burnett's career demonstrates the frequent interrelationship between children's and popular adult fiction. Like a significant number of other nineteenth-century writers, such as Maria Edgeworth, Captain Marryat, Charlotte Yonge, and Louisa May Alcott, Burnett wrote both kinds of fiction. Moreover, a study of how Burnett adapted character types and plot formulas from her love stories when she wrote for children points to the similarity of much children's and popular adult fiction to the folktale—despite touches of realism and the "new," both are formulaic, frankly fictive, and ultimately conservative; both favor a strong story line over complex, individualized characterization. Burnett's mastery of this kind of art goes a long way toward explaining the endurance of *Little Lord Fauntleroy* when other works which rode the crest of the late nineteenth-century sentimental cult of the child now seem impossibly dated, such as Margaret Finlay's Elsie Dinsmore books, Florence Montgomery's *Misunderstood,* and even, though to a lesser extent, the nursery stories of Mrs. Molesworth. The shared characteristics of much children's and popular adult fiction also suggest why both have proved highly adaptable to the twentieth-century mass medium of the film, notable examples being *The Wizard of Oz* and *Gone With the Wind,* as well as *Little Lord Fauntleroy.*

Obviously, Burnett will never approach in adult literature the primary place she has in children's literature. Her best books for children can still speak directly to a contemporary child reader; but to appreciate Burnett's adult fiction, most contemporary adult readers will have to make allowances for the time and in some cases the popular genre in which the books were written. Thus, as an adult writer Burnett is primarily of interest to the literary historian. This interest, however, is considerably greater than has been generally recognized. In reassessing the historical significance of Burnett's adult fiction, it is helpful to look first at some of the reasons for her critical decline during her lifetime and her near neglect after. Francis J. Molson identified the chief reasons in his 1975 call for a reassessment of Burnett: "a conviction that realism is inherently superior to romance," and especially popular romance, it should be added; "intense personal antipathy" to Burnett herself; and "opposition to Burnett's feminist stance."[1]

By abandoning her early efforts as a realist novelist and turning to romances, Burnett went against the mainstream of contemporary critical opinion as well as the mainline development of the novel toward realism, naturalism, psychological exploration, and formal experimentation. During the 1880s, Robert Louis Stevenson, whose *Treasure Island* (1883) would also become a children's classic, argued with some success for the aesthetic validity of the romance; but by the late 1890s, his opponents won the day and the romance was being largely relegated to the realm of popular literature. An increasing condescension toward books with popular appeal doubled the reasons Burnett's romances received short shrift from the critics. During the second half of the nineteenth century, as shown by surveys of the reading public by Q. D. Leavis, Amy Cruse, and James Hart,[2] the gap between "serious" and popular literature increased significantly. Earlier authors such as Dickens, Thackeray, Charlotte Brontë, and to a certain extent George Eliot had appealed to a wide audience as well as to professional readers. By the end of the century, however, many of the authors taken seriously by the critics were losing their appeal to a popular audience, sometimes because they offended conventional morality as did Thomas Hardy, and sometimes because their experimentation with the novel's form appealed to a more limited audience, as with Henry James.

At the same time, a host of professional writers—many of them women—were answering the needs of the popular reading public by using literary conventions and techniques that owed much to the earlier Dickens, Thackeray, C. Brontë, and Eliot. There was considerable resentment of these professional writers' financial success and of the personality cult which grew up around some of them in the popular press. Female writers were especially prone to attack, as suggested by the prevailing late nineteenth-century stereotype of the "lady novelist"—someone who pours forth a steady stream of mindless fiction the popularity of which gives its author an inflated sense of importance.

Burnett fit this stereotype all too easily with the prodigious popularity of her romances, her fondness for frills and furbelows, and her public posturing as the ideal mother portrayed in her children's fiction and, later, as the aristocratic "Romantick Lady"[3] like the heroines in her popular adult fiction. Attacked for her frivolous and self-serving public image, Burnett also offended many because much of her life and some of her fiction contradicted her ultrafeminine exterior. It was still slightly scandalous for a woman to live so long away from her husband and, often, her children and to keep company with an actor ten years her junior. And when Burnett paraded female nonconformity in the best-selling A Lady of Quality in 1896, her literary reputation began its long downward slide.

Indeed, Burnett's personality and life remain sufficiently provocative to elicit strong reactions likely to color one's evaluation of her literary achievement, especially in her popular adult romances. In 1951, Marghanita Laski made a long-overdue reassessment of Burnett's children's and adult fiction. In commenting on some biographical sources for her fiction, however, Laski warned that Burnett's books are best enjoyed if one knows "as little as possible about what they reveal of her own personality," for the Burnett unintentionally revealed in her son's biography is "aggressively domineering, offensively whimsical and abominably self-centered and conceited."[4] In her more sympathetic 1974 biography of Burnett, Ann Thwaite explored some of the private reasons for the public persona and isolated that in Burnett's personality which helps explain the course of her career. Thwaite suggests that Burnett's excessively romantic temperament urged her to escape unpleasant unrealities by trying to make her life a fairy tale; to earn the money necessary for this transformation, she wrote fairy tales for adults. Never quite able to forgive Burnett for turning from realist novels to popular romances, Thwaite says that her first best-seller, *Little Lord Fauntleroy*, changed Burnett from "a serious writer, striving to master an art, into a craftswoman who had the Midas touch," a "pen-driving machine" for "printing money."[5]

There is probably some justification for approaching Burnett's fiction through her biography. Like many prominent writers during her lifetime and after, she spent so much imaginative energy on her public image that it became another of her fictions; as such, this image is legitimately criticized as calculated, self-conscious, and often false as well as excessively "Romantick"—as *Little Lord Fauntleroy* sentimentalized the Romantic idealization of the child, Burnett's public image trivialized the Romantic deification of the artist. Recognition of certain tensions in Burnett's private life, however—her anxieties about economic security provoked by childhood poverty, and her unhappiness within marriage, as suggested by *Through One Administration*—allows one to understand if not entirely forgive her escape into the ultrafeminine romantic public image that gained her economic and social independence. More important, an awareness of how Burnett aggressively pursued her career and her nonconformist life-style under the cover of an ultrafeminine public exterior points to a similar strategy in much of her popular fiction. While allaying readers' anxieties about changing roles for women by adhering to the love story formula with its ending in a happy marriage, Burnett often expressed anger at male domination and suggested a more equitable balance of power between the two sexes.

Burnett's significance as a woman's writer can be indicated by a summary of some relevant themes in her realist fiction and popular and children's romances. A considerable number of her works portray the psychological and physical abuse or the unconscionable neglect of women by their fathers, lovers, or husbands. In *That Lass o' Lowrie's*, Joan's father beats her, there are references to wife-beating, and pregnant Liz is abandoned by her aristocratic lover. *A Woman's Will, A Lady of Quality*, and *The Shuttle* contain aristocratic women psychologically and physically broken by their husbands' alternate abuse and neglect. In *The Shuttle*, a man visualizes hanging his sister-in-law and cutting her into strips, and he later tries to rape her when she is alone and crippled by a fall from a horse.

Social conspiracy in constricting women's lives is suggested as well. *Through One Administration* portrays Bertha Amory's agonizing schizophrenia as she tries to cut herself to fit society's pattern for an obedient wife; and *The Making of a Marchioness, The Shuttle,* and *T. Tembarom* claim that high society often advertises women like soap and barters away their happiness. It should be added that Burnett's fiction exposes injustices not only in male and social control of women but also in insensitive adult authority over children, as in *The One I Knew the Best of All* and *A Little Princess.*

Burnett's anger at male domination is coupled with an exploration of female power in a variety of forms. The heroines of *A Lady of Quality* and *The Shuttle* use the traditionally male forms of power, physical force and money, to subdue men who have injured them or other women and to ameliorate this injury. Most of Burnett's women, however, use more traditionally female avenues of power. Some of her early magazine fiction and *The Pretty Sister of José* glory in the imperious power of the coquette. The childlike and ultrafeminine Dolly in *Vagabondia* and "Little Ann" in *T. Tembarom* manage their men's domestic and business affairs, and the heroines of *A Woman's Will* and *The Shuttle* extend their managerial skills to an entire country estate. Female friendships often help endure hardships and sometimes overcome the barriers of class and male interference, as in *That Lass o' Lowrie's, The Methods of Lady Walderhurst, The Shuttle,* and *A Little Princess.* And *The Pretty Sister of José, A Lady of Quality,* and *The Secret Garden* suggest supernatural sources of female power through references to the earth mother, Diana, and the Virgin and through portrayals of chains of female power including women long in the grave.

Finally, Burnett sometimes combined her sense of the injustice of male domination with her exaltation of female power to posit egalitarian marriage and less bifurcation between male and female roles. Fiction as varied as *Vagabondia, That Lass o' Lowrie's, Through One Administration, A Lady of Quality* and its sequel, and *The Shuttle* suggests that husbands should gracefully accept wives who possess managerial, economic, psychological, and even physical powers equal to or greater than their own. Female assumption of traditionally male powers and roles is also suggested by having women adopt male garb in "Seth" and *A Lady of Quality;* and Little Lord Fauntleroy may have become notorious partly because his androgyny threatened males using the models of Twain's rough-clad, smoking, and cussing boys, as Robert Lee White has suggested.[6]

Burnett owed much to other nineteenth-century women writers in her portrayal of female characters and themes. In *That Lass o' Lowrie's*, she used a female protagonist to explore social problems precipitated by industrialism, much as had Elizabeth Gaskell and Charlotte Brontë; and George Eliot and Gaskell provided notable precedents for Burnett's treatment of the fallen woman in Joan Lowrie's friend Liz. It is tempting to see at least a subterranean connection between Burnett's portrayal of a woman psychologically imprisoned by her husband in *Through One Administration* and the mad wife physically imprisoned by Rochester in *Jane Eyre*, since the women share the name of Bertha; the echoes of Jane Eyre in *The Secret Garden* have also been noted. *A Lady of Quality* owed much to the sensational fiction of the 1860s, such as Mary E. Braddon's *Lady Audley's Secret;* and many of Burnett's popular adult romances, as well as *The Secret Garden*, shared with late nineteenth-century feminist novelists an exaltation of female virtue and power.

Burnett, of course, did not limit her fiction to women and their concerns. She displayed a lifelong interest in the life-style and often the dialects peculiar to specific places. In America, she portrayed the rural south, New England, New York City, and Washington, D.C., offering her largest panorama of American society in *In Connection with The De Willoughby Claim*. Her British fiction compassed the industrial north, provincial towns, country estates, and London, and she set some of her minor short fiction in Paris and Italy. Probably Burnett's greatest contribution as a social documentarian, however, was her portrayal of social interchanges between America and Great Britain and her contrastive portrayal of the two societies, however idealized. Because of *A Fair Barbarian, Little Lord Fauntleroy, The Shuttle,* and *T. Tembarom,* as well as because of her own highly publicized life as an Anglo-American, Burnett stands foremost among the writers of the era who interpreted for a popular audience the international themes of Henry James.

Other contemporary themes in Burnett's fiction can also be noted briefly. Like much popular fiction written between 1870 and 1900, as Elmer F. Suderman has pointed out,[7] some of Burnett's romances show the impact of Darwin's theory of evolution. *In Connection with The De Willoughby Claim,* for example, posits a humanist replacement for Puritan theology, and some of her twentieth-century romances identify God as the impelling force of evolution. Burnett's involvement in theosophy and Christian Science resulted in two tales of the

occult, *In the Closed Room* and *The White People,* and surfaced in some
of her twentieth-century romances, including *The Secret Garden.* In
The Lost Prince, The Head of the House of Coombe, and *Robin* Burnett
approached World War I and twentieth-century social changes with
nostalgia for a royalist and aristocratic past, a nostalgia no doubt
shared by many whose personalities and values, like Burnett's, had
been shaped by the Victorian era. Such themes may have lost the appeal they had for a contemporary audience, but they illustrate the variety of issues Burnett addressed in her popular fiction.

Burnett proved versatile also in the fictional genres she attempted,
in addition to her writing for the stage; and a final review of her chief
fictional genres helps measure her achievement as an adult writer.
Ann Thwaite rates Burnett's early realist fiction too highly by claiming that had Burnett died "before she had written *Little Lord Fauntleroy,* she might well have had a reputation comparable to Mrs.
Gaskell's."[8] Burnett did equal Gaskell in capturing the working class
dialect of northern England; and, writing *That Lass o' Lowrie's*
twenty-four years after Gaskell's *Ruth,* Burnett was able to achieve a
more effective realist portrayal of the fallen woman—to argue against
social ostracism of such a woman, Gaskell had shown Ruth to be re-
pentant and pious, a paragon mother and social servant; but Burnett
could risk portraying a teenage mother resisting the preachments of
a self-righteous clergyman and neglecting the baby who has inter-
rupted her youthful dreams. Otherwise, however, Burnett almost always suffers by comparison to Gaskell. Her social vision in *That Lass
o' Lowrie's* is far narrower than in Gaskell's industrial novels, *Mary
Barton* and *North and South.* And Burnett's portrayal of life in a provincial English town in *A Fair Barbarian* lacks the subtlety of wit
and awareness of personal and social complexities of *Cranford.* Need-
less to say, Burnett did not match Dickens, from whom she borrowed
minor and often comic characters to underscore her social themes.
Nevertheless, Burnett's early British novels and short fiction deserve
some attention in studies of provincial and industrial themes in nineteenth-century British fiction.

Burnett's contributions to American realism are similarly notable
if not of the first rank. As in her British fiction, Burnett proved adept
at capturing just enough of a local dialect to make it seem authentic
but not too much to make it a barrier to a reader unacquainted with
it. While *Louisiana* must be accounted largely a failure in its use of
the American local color tradition, *In Connection with The De Wil-*

loughby Claim often proved effective, especially in its delineation of Southern rural life and character types. Without doubt, Burnett's most important contribution to American realism was *Through One Administration.* With her limited education and her exposure to the centers of power in Washington, D.C., largely that of a sociable wife, Burnett could not match the sophisticated portrayal of political intricacies in Henry Adams's *Democracy.* Similarly, she could not match the subtle portrayal of character and human relationships of her model Henry James, in large part because she could not completely transcend the typed characterization learned while writing popular romances and because she could not entirely confront the autobiographical sources of the novel. Though its flaws are painfully obvious when it is set beside the polished *Portrait of a Lady, Through One Administration* can be profitably read as a complementary picture of a nineteenth-century woman whose imagination and energies are tragically fettered by a failed marriage. Its main character the most complex in all of Burnett's fiction, *Through One Administration* best suggests Burnett's considerable potential as a realist novelist.

If Burnett's realist fiction never realized the potential of that genre, she frequently fulfilled and sometimes exceeded expectations appropriate to the popular romance. It was in this genre that Burnett made her best use of Dickens. Like him, she could often structure interrelated plots to include many characters from different geographical areas and social classes, as in *In Connection with The De Willoughby Claim, The Shuttle,* and *T. Tembarom.* Also, she proved adept at the Dickensian method of sketching in a typed character and then sustaining interest by showing that character in a series of slightly different situations, as especially in *Little Lord Fauntleroy* and *T. Tembarom.* Through its conflation of national with individual character types, *T. Tembarom* demonstrated Burnett's considerable talents in social comedy. And a comparison of how Burnett used the Cinderella tale as the basis for works as varied as some of her early love stories, *Little Lord Fauntleroy, The Making of a Marchioness, A Little Princess, The Secret Garden,* and *T. Tembarom,* shows Burnett's ingenuity in finding variations for familiar formulas, an essential talent for the successful writer of popular romance. While Burnett's longer romances often have effective passages and scenes, the short, lightly humorous *Making of a Marchioness* represents Burnett's most polished and lasting achievement in the popular adult romance. Its brevity checks the popular writer's impulse to address at length contemporary issues soon dated, and its light humor keeps at a safe distance the melo-drama endemic to popular fiction. What remains is that found in Burnett's best romances for children: a folktale revived with touches of realism and modern dress.

Burnett's decision to abandon her development as a realist novelist undoubtedly eclipsed any chance she may have had to make a lasting name for herself in the "world of actual literature," as she once put it.[9] And her subsequent adherence to the safe conservatism of love romance formulas may have kept her from being the pioneer in the female literary tradition she might otherwise have been. Of the chil-dren's and popular adult romance, however, she became a master; she deserves a primary place in the annals of children's and popular literature.

Notes and References

Preface

1. Francis J. Molson, "Frances Hodgson Burnett (1848–1924)," *American Literary Realism* 8 (Winter 1975):36.
2. John G. Cawelti, *Adventure, Mystery, and Romance: Formula Stories as Art and Popular Culture* (Chicago: University of Chicago Press, 1976), p. 9; as indicated by this preface, I am much indebted to Cawelti for the critical approach to Burnett's popular fiction in my subsequent chapters.
3. Ibid., p. 16.
4. Elaine Showalter, *A Literature of Their Own: British Women Novelists from Brontë to Lessing* (Princeton: Princeton University Press, 1977), p. 154.
5. Molson, "Frances Hodgson Burnett."

Chapter One

1. "Literary Spotlight," *Bookman* 56 (October 1922):158–62; quoted in Molson, "Frances Hodgson Burnett," p. 37.
2. For most of the information in this chapter, as well as biographical information in subsequent chapters, I am indebted to Ann Thwaite, *Waiting for the Party: The Life of Frances Hodgson Burnett 1849–1924* (New York, 1974).
3. Quoted in Vivian Burnett, *The Romantick Lady, (Frances Hodgson Burnett): The Life Story of an Imagination* (New York, 1927), p. 51.
4. *The One I Knew the Best of All,* chap. 8; hereafter cited in the text as *O.*
5. Burnett called herself "The Romantick Lady" in a self-conscious, autobiographical series of essays for *Good Housekeeping,* 1914–16, 1920.
6. Constance Buel Burnett, *Happily Ever After: A Portrait of Frances Hodgson Burnett* (New York: Vanguard, 1969) is based primarily on *The One I Knew the Best of All* and Burnett, *The Romantick Lady.*
7. Quoted in Burnett, *Romantick Lady,* p. 47.
8. Quoted in Thwaite, *Waiting for the Party,* p. 52.
9. *Boston Transcript,* quoted ibid., p. 56.
10. The precise number of plays Burnett wrote and their complete production history remain to be established; most are not available in published form. The primary task of this study is to survey Burnett's large body of fiction; however, a general history of her theater career based on information in Thwaite will be included in this chapter.
11. Quoted ibid., p. 60.

12. Charles Scribner described Burnett thus to Frederick Warne, his British publishing counterpart, quoted ibid., p. 55.

13. James Herbert Morse, "The Native Element in American Fiction Since the War," *Century* 27 (July 1883):362–75.

14. Quoted in Thwaite, *Waiting for the Party,* pp. 87, 66–67.

15. *Through One Administration,* chap. 24.

16. Quoted in Thwaite, *Waiting for the Party,* p. 80.

17. In *Piccino and Other Child Stories.*

18. Thwaite, *Waiting for the Party,* p. 108.

19. James D. Hart, *The Popular Book: A History of America's Literary Taste* (1950; reprint ed., Berkeley: University of California Press, 1963), p. 187.

20. Letter from Burnett to a cousin, quoted in Thwaite, *Waiting for the Party,* p. 134.

21. Letter from Burnett to a friend, quoted ibid., p. 122.

22. Letter from Burnett to a friend, quoted ibid., p. 109.

23. Quoted ibid., pp. 112, 116.

24. Quoted in Burnett, *Romantick Lady,* p. 138.

25. Quoted in Thwaite, *Waiting for the Party,* pp. 119, 146.

26. Quoted ibid., pp. 152–53, 175.

27. Molson, "Frances Hodgson Burnett," p. 37.

28. Quoted in Thwaite, *Waiting for the Party,* pp. 177–78, 190.

29. Ibid., pp. 190–92.

30. Ibid., pp. 180, 215.

31. Ibid., pp. 216, 240.

32. From a contemporary account quoted ibid., p. 61.

33. Quoted ibid., pp. 229, 244.

34. Quoted ibid., pp. 201–2.

35. *New York World* critic quoted ibid., p. 218.

36. Ibid., p. 254.

37. Quoted ibid., pp. 225, 240.

38. Quoted ibid., p. 236.

39. Quoted in Burnett, *Romantick Lady,* p. 410.

Chapter Two

1. Quoted in Burnett, *Romantick Lady,* pp. 64, 51.

2. Both in *Earlier Stories.*

3. In *Surly Tim and Other Stories.*

4. In *Natalie and Other Stories.*

5. Ibid.

6. In *Surly Tim.*

7. Ibid.

8. In *Our Neighbor Opposite* (London, 1878), pp. 160, 146.

9. In *Surly Tim.*

10. In *Natalie.*

11. In *Surly Tim.*

12. Ibid.

13. *Vagabondia: A Love Story* (New York, 1883); hereafter cited in the text.

14. Review of *Dolly, Nation,* 24 January 1878, p. 66.

15. Burnett, *Romantick Lady,* pp. 48–50.

16. *Nation,* 24 January 1878, p. 66.

17. Quoted in Burnett, *Romantick Lady,* p. 120.

18. Thwaite, *Waiting for the Party,* p. 74.

19. *The One I Knew the Best of All,* chap. 5.

20. *That Lass o' Lowrie's* (New York, 1877), p. 1; hereafter cited in the text.

21. Letter to Richard Watson Gilder, quoted in Burnett, *Romantick Lady,* p. 70.

22. *Nation,* 19 July 1877, p. 44.

23. *Atlantic Monthly,* November 1877, p. 631.

24. Letter to Richard Watson Gilder, quoted in Burnett, *Romantick Lady,* p. 84.

25. *Harper's New Monthly Magazine,* November 1879, p. 955.

26. *Haworth's* (New York, 1879), p. 336.

27. Burnett, *Romantick Lady,* pp. 105–6.

28. Thwaite, *Waiting for the Party,* p. 69.

29. *Louisiana* (New York, 1880), pp. 162–63.

30. Burnett, *Romantick Lady,* p. 98.

31. *A Fair Barbarian* (Boston, 1881), p. 38; hereafter cited in the text.

32. Quoted in Burnett, *Romantick Lady,* p. 91.

33. Review of *Through One Administration, Nation,* 28 June 1883, p. 552.

34. Ibid., and review of *Through One Administration, Athenaeum,* 12 May 1883, p. 600.

35. *Athenaeum,* 12 May 1883, p. 600.

36. "American Fiction by Women," *Atlantic Monthly,* July 1883, p. 123.

37. Quoted in Thwaite, *Waiting for the Party,* p. 77.

38. Ibid., pp. 76–78.

39. Quoted ibid., pp. 51–52.

40. Burnett, *Romantick Lady,* pp. 120–21.

41. *Hamlet,* 1. 5. 188.

42. According to Thwaite, *Waiting for the Party,* pp. 51, 98, Burnett named her son Vivian, whom she had hoped would be a girl, after Merlin's seducer in *Idylls of the King;* Tennyson later returned the compliment by tell-

ing one of Burnett's friends that a certain passage in *Through One Adminis-tration*, now unidentified, was "the finest piece of English he had ever seen."
43. *The Literary History of the United States*, ed. Robert E. Spiller et al., 4th rev. ed. (New York: Macmillan, 1974), p. 277, mentions Burnett only once in the history—in a section describing the sale of American books in Germany, Burnett is listed as one of the most often translated; in the bibliography volume of this history, *Through One Administration* is listed with *The Gilded Age, Democracy*, and several other political novels of the time. Alexander Cowie, in *The Rise of the American Novel* (New York: American Book Company, 1948), devotes twenty-six pages to Harriet Beecher Stowe and ten pages to Constance Fenimore Woolson, but ignores Burnett completely.

Chapter Three

1. Cawelti, *Adventure*, p. 261.
2. Burnett, *Romantick Lady*, pp. 135–36.
3. Ibid., p. 105, Burnett says that his mother had a "habit" "to slip in a short 'easy' book between big ones."
4. Preface to *Giovanni and the Other Children Who Have Made Stories* (New York, 1892), p. vii; hereafter cited in the text as *G*.
5. "How Fauntleroy Occurred," in *Piccino and Other Child Stories* (New York, 1894) pp. 198–99; hereafter cited in the text as *P*.
6. Thwaite, *Waiting for the Party*, pp. 92, 118, 120.
7. Quoted in Burnett, *Romantick Lady*, p. 138.
8. Thwaite, *Waiting for the Party*, pp. 116, 112.
9. "Sara Crewe" will be discussed more fully in the analysis of *A Little Princess* in the next chapter.
10. *St. Nicholas* 15 (January 1889):208.
11. In *Giovanni and the Other*.
12. "*Two Little Pilgrims' Progress:* The 1893 Chicago Columbian Exposition as Celestial City," *Markham Review* 7 (Spring 1978):55–59.
13. Quoted in Thwaite, *Waiting for the Party*, p. 144.
14. Ibid., p. 103; in *The Head of the House of Coombe*, Burnett has a child's nurse reading *Lady Audley's Secret*.
15. Showalter, *A Literature of Their Own*, pp. 164–65; Winifred Hughes, *The Maniac in the Cellar: Sensation Novels of the 1860s* (Princeton: Princeton University Press, 1980).
16. Burnett, *Romantick Lady*, p. 151.
17. Quoted in Thwaite, *Waiting for the Party*, p. 127.
18. *The Pretty Sister of José* (New York, 1889), p. 24; hereafter cited in the text.
19. Thwaite, *Waiting for the Party*, p. 181.
20. Burnett read several books by Yonge in 1887 when she read many

of Braddon's works; it is probable, however, that she had read *The Heir of Redclyffe* earlier, since its immense popularity began immediately after its publication in 1853.

21. *Miss Defarge*, with John Habberton, *Brueton's Bayou* (Philadelphia, 1888), p. 167.

22. *A Lady of Quality* (New York, 1896), p. 363; hereafter cited in the text.

23. *Athenaeum*, 4 April 1896, p. 440.

24. *Nation*, 21 May 1896, p. 398.

25. *A Lady of Quality* is nevertheless listed by Gene Damon and Lee Stuart in *The Lesbian in Literature: A Bibliography* (San Francisco: Daughters of Bilitis, 1967), p. 11; Burnett's romance is put in the category of works indicating "latent, repressed Lesbianism or characters who can be so interpreted. This type of behavior is properly termed 'variant' behavior" (p. 1).

26. *Atlantic Monthly*, August 1896, p. 275.

27. Quoted in Burnett, *Romantick Lady*, p. 249.

28. Quoted ibid., pp. 249–50.

29. Cawelti, *Adventure*, pp. 261–62.

30. *In Connection with The De Willoughby Claim* (New York, 1899), p. 296; hereafter cited in the text.

31. Quoted in Burnett, *Romantick Lady*, pp. 409–10.

32. *Nation*, 29 March 1900, p. 245; *Athenaeum*, 6 January 1900, p. 9.

Chapter Four

1. *Two Little Pilgrims' Progress* (New York, 1895), p. 191.

2. "The Troubles of Queen Silver Bell," *St. Nicholas* 33 (October 1906):1065.

3. *The Land of the Blue Flower* (New York, 1909), p. 22; hereafter cited in the text.

4. Burnett, *Romantick Lady*, p. 374.

5. In "The Romantick Lady," *Good Housekeeping* 60 (March 1915):359, Burnett said that "apart from the mere forms, which are individual matters," she believed what is believed by the Jews, Catholics, Methodists, Episcopalians, Presbyterians, Unitarians, Buddhists, Brahmins, pupils of Confucius, and had her "own belief besides."

6. Burnett, *Romantick Lady*, p. 377.

7. *The Dawn of a To-morrow* (New York, 1906), pp. 100–101, 129.

8. *The White People* (New York, 1917), p. 27; hereafter cited in the text.

9. "The tale is there, not to hide, but to show: if it show nothing at your window, do not open your door to it; leave it out in the cold" (George

MacDonald, "The Fantastic Imagination," in *The Gifts of the Child Christ,* ed. Glenn Edward Sadler, 2 vols. [Grand Rapids: Eerdmans, 1973], 1:28).

10. "The First Knife in the World," *St. Nicholas* 37 (December 1909):101; hereafter cited in the text.

11. Burnett, *Romantick Lady,* p. 410.

12. "New Novels," *Athenaeum,* 14 December 1901, p. 807.

13. Cawelti, *Adventure,* pp. 12–13.

14. Ibid., pp. 16–20.

15. Letter to V. Burnett, 17 February 1901, quoted in Burnett, *Romantick Lady,* p. 301.

16. Quoted ibid.

17. *The Making of a Marchioness* (New York, 1901), p. 182; hereafter cited in the text.

18. Cawelti, *Adventure,* p. 12.

19. Thwaite, *Waiting for the Party,* p. 198.

20. *The Methods of Lady Walderhurst* (New York, 1901), p. 62.

21. Thwaite, *Waiting for the Party,* p. 202.

22. Iona and Peter Opie, *The Classic Fairy Tales* (London: Oxford University Press, 1974), pp. 12–14.

23. Thwaite, *Waiting for the Party,* pp. 192–93.

24. *The Shuttle* (New York, 1907), p. 1; hereafter cited in the text.

25. Thwaite, *Waiting for the Party,* pp. 217, 192.

26. Ibid., p. 216.

27. Letter to a friend, 19 August 1906, quoted in Burnett, *Romantick Lady,* p. 321.

28. "It was a habit of Frances' to slip in a short 'easy' book between big ones" (Burnett, *Romantick Lady,* p. 105).

29. Thwaite, *Waiting for the Party,* p. 181.

30. Many of my comments about *The Secret Garden* as well as, earlier, about *Little Lord Fauntleroy* and *A Little Princess,* first appeared in Phyllis Bixler Koppes, "Tradition and the Individual Talent of Frances Hodgson Burnett," *Children's Literature* 7 (1978):191–207.

31. In "Aschenputtel," collected by the brothers Grimm, the heroine plants a hazel tree on the grave of her mother; a bird which perches on the tree later gives her her wishes (Opie, *The Classic Fairy Tales,* p. 118).

32. *Faerie Queene,* 3. 6. 47.

33. 1805. 13.100; 2. 271.

34. Thwaite, *Waiting for the Party,* p. 220.

35. Sandra M. Gilbert and Susan Gubar, *The Madwoman in the Attic: The Woman in the Nineteenth Century Literary Imagination* (New Haven: Yale University Press, 1979), p. xi.

36. Showalter, *A Literature of Their Own,* pp. 190, 185.

37. *In the Garden* (Boston, 1925), pp. 14–15, 19; hereafter cited in the text.

38. Burnett, *Romantick Lady,* p. 403.

39. "The Passing of the Kings," *Good Housekeeping* 68 (March 1919):10–11; hereafter cited in the text.

40. Thwaite, *Waiting for the Party,* p. 232.

41. Ibid., p. 169.

42. *The Head of the House of Coombe* (New York, 1922), pp. 211, 208, 207; hereafter cited in the text as *C.*

43. *Robin* (New York, 1922), pp. 9–10; hereafter cited in the text as *R.*

44. Thwaite, *Waiting for the Party,* p. 241.

45. Frances Hodgson Burnett, quoted in Burnett, *Romantick Lady,* p. 51.

46. Quoted in Thwaite, *Waiting for the Party,* p. 240.

Chapter Five

1. Molson, "Frances Hodgson Burnett," p. 41.

2. Q. D. Leavis, *Fiction and the Reading Public* (1912; reprint ed., London: Chatto & Windus, 1965); Amy Cruse, *The Victorians and Their Books* (1935; reprint ed., London: Allen & Unwin, 1962); Hart, *The Popular Book.*

3. Burnett called herself "the Romantick Lady" in a self-conscious series of essays for *Good Housekeeping* in 1914–16 and 1920; her son also used this description in the title of his 1927 biography.

4. Marghanita Laski, *Mrs. Ewing, Mrs. Molesworth, and Mrs. Hodgson Burnett* (New York, 1951), pp. 78, 77.

5. Thwaite, *Waiting for the Party,* p. 86.

6. Robert Lee White, "Little Lord Fauntleroy as Hero," in *Challenges in American Culture,* ed. Ray B. Browne et al. (Bowling Green, 1970), pp. 209–16.

7. Elmer F. Suderman, "Popular Fiction (1870–1900) Looks at Darwin and the Nature of God," ibid., pp. 142–49.

8. Thwaite, *Waiting for the Party,* p. 240.

9. Quoted in *Romantick Lady,* Burnett, p. 51.

Selected Bibliography

PRIMARY SOURCES

Most of Burnett's fiction first appeared in periodicals. Periodical publication is listed only when it preceded book publication by three or more years or when periodical publication must be consulted to read a work in its entirety, as in the Queen Crosspatch Series. When it was not possible to view the first editions, publication information was taken from the bibliography in Ann Thwaite's *Waiting for the Party*.

1. Fiction and Drama for Children

Barty Crusoe and His Man Saturday. New York: Moffat Yard, 1909.

"Editha's Burglar." *St. Nicholas* 7 (February 1880):326–32. *Editha's Burglar: A Story for Children.* Boston: Jordan Marsh, 1888.

"The First Knife in the World." *St. Nicholas* 37 (December 1909):99–105.

Giovanni and the Other Children Who Have Made Stories. New York: Scribner's, 1892. As *Children I Have Known.* London: J. R. Osgood; London: McIlvaine, 1892.

The Good Wolf. New York: Moffat Yard, 1908.

The Land of the Blue Flower. New York: Moffat Yard, 1909; London: Putnam, 1912.

Little Lord Fauntleroy. New York: Scribner's; London: Warne, 1886. Facsimile of Scribner's 1886 edition, preface by Ann Thwaite. New York and London: Garland, 1976.

Little Lord Fauntleroy: A Drama in Three Acts Founded on The Story of the Same Name. New York and London: Samuel French, 1889.

Little Saint Elizabeth and Other Stories. New York: Scribner's; London: Warne, 1890.

A Little Princess: Being the Whole Story of Sara Crewe Now Told for the First Time. New York Scribner's; London: Warne, 1905.

The Little Princess: A Play for Children and Grown-up Children in Three Acts. New York and London: Samuel French, 1911.

The Lost Prince. New York: Century; London: Hodder & Stoughton, 1915.

Piccino and Other Child Stories. New York: Scribner's, 1894. As *The Captain's Youngest.* London: Warne, 1894.

The Queen Crosspatch Series. "The Troubles of Queen Silver Bell," *St. Nicholas* 33 (October 1906):1059–67; New York: Century, 1906; London: Warne, 1907. "How Winnie Hatched the Little Rooks," *St.*

Nicholas 34 (November 1906):3–12. "Racketty-Packetty House," *St. Nicholas* 34 (December 1906–January 1907):97–106, 195–203; New York: Century, 1906; London: Warne, 1907. "The Cozy Lion," *St. Nicholas* 34 (February–March 1907):291–98, 387–94; New York: Century, 1907. "The Spring Cleaning," *St. Nicholas* 36 (December 1908–January 1909):99–104, 242–48; New York: Century, 1908.

Sara Crewe and Editha's Burglar. London: Warne, 1888.

Sara Crewe, Little Saint Elizabeth and Other Stories. New York: Scribner's, 1897.

The Secret Garden. New York: Stokes; London: Heinemann, 1911.

Two Little Pilgrims' Progress: A Story of the City Beautiful. New York: Scribner's; London: Warne, 1895.

The Way to the House of Santa Claus: A Christmas Story for Very Small Boys in Which Every Little Reader Is the Hero of a Big Adventure. New York: Harper, 1916.

2. Autobiography, Fiction, and Drama for Adults

In the Closed Room. New York: Grosset & Dunlap; London: Hodder & Stoughton, 1904.

In Connection with The De Willoughby Claim. New York: Scribner's; London: Warne, 1899.

The Dawn of a To-morrow. New York: Scribner's, 1906; London: Warne, 1907.

Earlier Stories: First Series. New York: Scribner's, 1878; London: Routledge, 1879.

Earlier Stories: Second Series. New York: Scribner's, 1878; London: Chatto, 1879.

Esmeralda: A Comedy Drama in Four Acts. New York and London: Samuel French, 1909. With William Gillette.

A Fair Barbarian. Boston: Osgood; London: Warne, 1881.

"The Fortunes of Philippa Fairfax," *Semi-Weekly Inter Ocean* (Chicago) 13 (October 4–November 22 1886); London: Warne, 1888.

Haworth's. New York: Scribner's; London: Macmillan, 1879.

The Head of the House of Coombe. New York: Stokes; London: Heinemann, 1922.

His Grace of Osmonde: Being the Portions of That Nobleman's Life Omitted in the Relation of His Lady's Story Presented to the World of Fashion Under the Title of A Lady of Quality. New York: Scribner's; London: Warne, 1897.

Jarl's Daughter and Other Stories and Other Novelettes. Philadelphia: Peterson, 1879.

Kathleen. Philadelphia: Peterson; London: Routledge, 1878.

A Lady of Quality: Being a Most Curious, Hitherto Unknown History, as Related by Mr. Isaac Bickerstaff But Not Presented to the World of Fashion Through the Pages of the Tattler and Now for the First Time Written Down. New York: Scribner's; London: Warne, 1896.

That Lass o' Lowrie's. New York: Scribner; London: Warne, 1877.

The Little Hunchback Zia. New York: Stokes; London, Heinemann, 1916.

Louisiana. New York: Scribner's, 1880. With *That Lass o' Lowrie's.* London: Macmillan, 1880.

The Making of a Marchioness. New York: Stokes; London: Smith Elder, 1901.

The Methods of Lady Walderhurst. New York: Stokes, 1901; London: Smith Elder, 1902.

Miss Crespigny. Philadelphia: Peterson; London: Routledge, 1878; New York: Scribner's, 1879.

Natalie and Other Stories. London: Warne, 1879.

Our Neighbor Opposite. London: Routledge, 1878.

The One I Knew the Best of All: A Memory of the Mind of a Child. New York: Scribner's; London: Warne, 1893. Facsimile of 1893 Warne edition. London: William Clowes, 1974. Reprint of 1893 edition: New York: Arno, 1980.

Pretty Polly Pemberton. Philadelphia: Peterson, 1877; London: Routledge, 1878.

The Pretty Sister of José. New York: Scribner's; London: Spencer Blackett, 1889.

A Quiet Life and The Tide on the Moaning Bar. Philadelphia: Peterson, 1878; London: Routledge, 1879.

Robin. New York: Stokes; London: Heinemann, 1922.

The Shuttle. New York: Stokes; London: Heinemann, 1907.

Surly Tim and Other Stories. New York: Scribner; Toronto: Robertsons; London: Ward Lock, 1877.

Theo. Philadelphia: Peterson; London: Ward Lock; London: Warne, 1877; New York: Scribner, 1879.

Through One Administration. Boston: Osgood; London: Warne, 1883. Reprint of 1883 edition, introduction by Robert Lee White. New York: Johnson Reprint, 1969.

T. Tembarom. New York: Stokes; London: Hodder & Stoughton, 1913.

Vagabondia: A Love Story. New York: Scribner's, 1883; Boston: Osgood, 1884. As *Dolly,* without Burnett's revision and correction. Philadelphia: Porter & Coates; London: Routledge, 1877.

The White People. New York: Harper, 1917; London: Heinemann, 1920.

A Woman's Will. London: Warne, 1887. As *Miss Defarge,* with John Habberton, *Brueton's Bayou.* Philadelphia: Lippincott, 1888.

3. Selected Essays

"A City of Groves and Bowers." *St. Nicholas* 20 (June 1893):563–71.

The Drury Lane Boys' Club. Washington, D.C.: The Moon, 1892.

In the Garden. Boston: Medici Society, 1925.

Kate Douglas Wiggen: A Sketch of Her Life. Boston: Old Corner Book Store, [1924].

My Robin. New York: Stokes, 1912; London: Putnam, 1913.

"The Passing of the Kings." *Good Housekeeping* 68 (March 1919):10–12, 118–28.

The Romantick Lady Series. "The Christmas in the Fog," *Good Housekeeping* 59 (December 1914):661–71; "The Woman in the Other Stateroom," *Good Housekeeping* 60 (March 1915):357–68; "The Attic in the House on Long Island," *Good Housekeeping* 62 (May 1916):549–59; "The House in the Dismal Swamp," *Good Housekeeping* 70 (April 1920):16–18.

"When He Decides." In *Before He Is Twenty: Five Perplexing Phases of the Boy Question Considered.* New York: Fleming Revell, 1894. With Mrs. Lyman Abbot, Edward W. Bok, Robert J. Burdette, Mrs. Burton Harrison.

4. Manuscripts

Manuscript materials relevant to Burnett's life and career are held by many libraries in the United States and England, and there is no comprehensive guide to these holdings; the Scribner Archives in the Princeton University Library have much of her professional correspondence.

SECONDARY SOURCES

1. Biographies

Burnett, Constance Buel. *Happily Ever After: A Portrait of Frances Hodgson Burnett.* New York: Vanguard, 1969. Intended to appeal to children, is based primarily on *The One I Knew the Best of All* and V. Burnett, *The Romantick Lady.*

Burnett, Vivian. *The Romantick Lady (Frances Hodgson Burnett): The Life Story of an Imagination.* New York: Charles Scribner's Sons, 1927. Adulatory biography by Burnett's son. The only published source for some of her personal and professional correspondence and some of her life.

Thwaite, Ann. *Waiting for the Party: The Life of Frances Hodgson Burnett 1849–1924.* New York: Charles Scribner's Sons, 1974. The most complete biography, based on considerable research in Great Britain and the United States. Surveys Burnett's writing and theatrical career primarily as it reveals her personality and life. Finds her excessively romantic and pathetically unrealized as an artist. Contains a bibliography of her plays in both Great Britain and the United States.

2. Critical Studies

Bixler, Phyllis. "Idealization of the Child and Childhood in Frances Hodgson Burnett's *Little Lord Fauntleroy* and Mark Twain's *Tom Sawyer*." In *Research About Nineteenth-Century Children and Books: Portrait Studies*, edited by Selma K. Richardson. Urbana: University of Illinois Graduate School of Library Science, 1980, pp. 85–96. Relates *Little Lord Fauntleroy* to Romantic concepts of the child and pastoral tradition in nineteenth-century children's literature.

————. "*Little Lord Fauntleroy*: Continuity and Change in Popular Entertainment." In *Children's Novels and the Movies*, edited by Douglas Street. New York: Frederick Ungar, 1983, pp. 69–80. Compares Burnett's romance and stage adaptation with subsequent film versions, especially David O. Selznick's 1936 film and Norman Rosemont's 1980 movie for television.

————. "The Oral-Formulaic Training of a Popular Fiction Writer: Frances Hodgson Burnett." *Journal of Popular Culture* 15 (Spring 1982):42–52. Notes Burnett's use of popular fiction formulas to compose stories orally as a child, suggesting some similarities between oral narrative and popular fiction.

Gohlke, Madelon S. "Rereading *The Secret Garden*." *College English* 41 (April 1980):894–902. Focuses on the themes of illness and health in the book as Gohlke describes its powerful impact on her during a childhood illness. Uses a comparison of her childhood and adulthood responses to the book to analyze the process of literary interpretation.

Heywood, Christopher. "Frances Hodgson Burnett's *The Secret Garden*: A Possible Source for T. S. Eliot's 'Rose Garden.' " *Yearbook of English Studies* 7 (1977):166–71. Like Alison White, q. v., identifies Burnett's book as the unacknowledged source for the rose garden and its childhood associations in T. S. Eliot's *Burnt Norton*. Also finds possible echoes of the same in *The Family Reunion*, *The Confidential Clerk*, and *Marina*.

Keyser, Elizabeth Lennox. " 'Quite Contrary': Frances Hodgson Burnett's *The Secret Garden*." *Children's Literature* 11 (1983):1–13. Argues that Burnett's own "ambivalence about sex roles" led to her unsuccessful attempt to glorify Colin at the expense of Mary near the end of the book.

Koppes, Phyllis Bixler. "Tradition and the Individual Talent of Frances Hodgson Burnett: A Generic Analysis of *Little Lord Fauntleroy*, *A Little Princess*, and *The Secret Garden*." *Children's Literature: An International Journal* 7 (1978):191–207. A comparative analysis of the three books showing Burnett's use of the fairy tale, the exemplum, the Romantic concept of the child, and the literary pastoral tradition.

Laski, Marghanita. *Mrs. Ewing, Mrs. Molesworth and Mrs. Hodgson Burnett*. New York: Oxford University Press, 1951. Identifies some biographical sources for Burnett's fiction. Discusses some of Burnett's adult fiction, complimenting the portrayal of industrial life in her Lancashire novels but calling *The Making of a Marchioness* "most people's favorite." Says that *Little Lord Fauntleroy, A Little Princess,* and *The Secret Garden* "represent all that is important in Mrs. Burnett's contribution to children's literature" and that *Little Lord Fauntleroy* "is the best version of the Cinderella story in modern idiom."

Molson, Francis J. "Frances Hodgson Burnett (1848–1924)." *American Literary Realism* 8 (Winter, 1975):35–41. Surveys Burnett's reception during her lifetime and after. Cites some reasons for her critical decline. While admitting that she is an author of "secondary" importance, claims that "her writing deserves better than the almost total neglect it has received." Cites available editions and reprints and some of the many libraries in the United States with manuscript holdings.

————. "*Two Little Pilgrims' Progress:* The 1893 Chicago Columbian Exposition as Celestial City." *Markham Review* 7 (Spring 1978):55–59. Discusses the book as a secularization of John Bunyan's Christian allegory, in which "heaven" is defined as the fruits of the American work ethic, energy, and ingenuity.

White, Alison. "Tap-Roots into a Rose Garden." *Children's Literature* 1 (1972):74–76. Identifies *The Secret Garden* as the unacknowledged source for the rose garden in T. S. Eliot's *Burnt Norton.*

White, Robert Lee. "Little Lord Fauntleroy as Hero." In *Challenges in American Culture,* edited by Ray B. Browne, Larry N. Landrum, and William Bottorff. Bowling Green: Bowling Green University Popular Press, 1970, pp. 209–16. Argues that Little Lord Fauntleroy's reputation as a "prissy 'mollycoddle' " was unfair to Burnett's book and arose partly because American males preferred Twain's Huck Finn as a model. Discusses Stephen Crane's disdain for Burnett's book and cites Ernest Hemingway and Hart Crane as examples of how the Huck Finn model of American masculinity could prove destructive.

Index